THE
QUESTION
IS COLLEGE

INNOVATORS IN EDUCATION
SERIES EDITOR: SUSANNAH SHEFFER

The *Innovators in Education* series brings back into print books that are both historically significant and that speak directly to today's concerns. We look for books that represent important developments in educational thought and have ongoing contemporary application. In this way, the series enables readers to connect newly published books with earlier works on similar subjects and enables current discussions to be informed and enriched by some of the best available writing on educational issues.

Also available in the series:
Daniel Fader, *The Naked Children*
James Herndon, *How to Survive in Your Native Land*
James Herndon, *The Way It Spozed to Be*
John Holt, *What Do I Do Monday?*
John Holt, *Freedom and Beyond*
Herbert Kohl, *Reading, How To*
Ken Macrorie, *Uptaught*

HERBERT KOHL

THE QUESTION IS COLLEGE

ON FINDING AND DOING WORK YOU LOVE

Series Editor
SUSANNAH SHEFFER

Boynton/Cook Publishers

HEINEMANN

Portsmouth, NH

Boynton/Cook Publishers, Inc.
A subsidiary of Reed Elsevier Inc.
361 Hanover Street
Portsmouth, NH 03801-3912
http://www.heinemann.com

Offices and agents throughout the world

This book was previously published by Random House in 1989 as *The
Question Is College: Guiding Your Child to the Right Choices After High
School* by Herbert Kohl.

We would like to thank those who have given their permission to include
material in this book.

Library of Congress Cataloging-in-Publication Data
CIP is on file with the Library of Congress.
ISBN 0-86709-434-6

Editor: Susannah Sheffer
Cover design: Barbara Werden
Cover photo: Monica Menduno
Manufacturing: Courtney Ordway

Printed in the United States of America on acid-free paper
02 01 00 99 98   DA   1 2 3 4 5

CONTENTS

FOREWORD TO THE
NEW EDITION

What do I really care about? What do I want to do with my life? Such burning questions occupy the minds of young people—or would, if we gave them half a chance. But we occupy them instead with questions of getting into a good college and finding a good job. As Herbert Kohl points out, "Exploration of young people's interests and talents is not part of the usual school curriculum." No wonder so many young people see work more in terms of its eventual benefits than in terms of the intrinsic meaning or satisfaction it might offer.

In the late 1970s, the writer and educator John Holt recalled talking to a group of students about the difference between jobs, careers, and work. A job, Holt said, was something you did for money, "something someone else told you to do and paid you to do." A career was a succession of such jobs, each presumably with increasing pay, responsibility, and prestige. Work, on the other hand was:

> something altogether different, what people used to call a "vocation" or "calling"—something that seemed so worth doing for its own sake that they would have gladly chosen to do it even if they didn't need the money and the work didn't pay. I went on to say that to find our work, in this sense, is one of the most important and difficult tasks that we have in life.

Twenty years ago, most of the students in Holt's audience found his notion of work "not just impossible, but unimaginable." I think it's likely that the same is true of many or even most students today. But in *The Question is College*, Kohl persists in raising the question of vocation and in believing that there lurks even within today's young people a hunger for this question, though they may be scared of or discouraged from admitting it. *The Question is College* is about growing up—which is to say, about finding out how you will connect with the world, move through that world, make a place for yourself within it. It's about figuring out what you love so much that you would do it without thought of reward.

How does college enter in? Kohl questions college because college is nowadays presumed to be the only, or at any rate the best, route to adulthood. He isn't opposed to college categorically; he's opposed to going without thinking, without having reason, without having first asked oneself the question about what one really wants from life. He recognizes that there are students who resist this automatic, unthinking procession into higher education.

From my own discussions with young people, I know that Kohl is onto something. "I don't know how to tell my parents that I'm not sure I want to go to college next year," says a child in a middle class academic family, the sort of family in which it's assumed that children will go to college just as they'll grow taller and get driver's licenses. What is such a young person saying? That she's not sure it's right to spend all that money on college when she isn't yet convinced it's the best choice for her? That she isn't ready, at so young an age, to submit to the notion that there is only one path? That she isn't sure whether, or how, college will contribute to the process of finding out what she really wants to do, and that her hunger, especially after so many years of schooling, is for a taste of the real world and a glimpse of what people actually do in it?

Kohl knows how to listen to young people and to hear the deeper beliefs or fears or passions that underlie comments that may sound like belligerence or aimlessness. In fact, he makes it clear that if he hadn't listened to young people—his own children included—he might not have learned enough to write this book. But he has. With extraordinary sensitivity to generational differences, Kohl allowed himself to realize that his children's lives were simply not the same as his own had been at their age. He listened to the students who had plans or dreams that didn't include college and students who had no idea what they dreamed of but wanted a chance to find out. The book ends up being a powerful discussion of how to navigate generational differences and how to survive when children don't meet their parents' expectations. No matter how many time I read Kohl's stories of parents cutting off communication with their children for deciding against college, I find them heartbreaking. Don't be more committed to your expectations than to your children, Kohl is saying.

The young people Kohl listens to are speaking from a deep part of themselves, the part that knows growing up is about something more than doing what everyone else says you're supposed to do. Finding a vocation is an old-fashioned notion, now so obscured by contemporary pressures that it actually strikes us as radical and new—and so very welcome. The years when *The Question is College* was out of print were barren ones; I had to keep summarizing it for families and telling them wistfully that someday it might come back into print. Now it has, and a new group of readers can benefit from its wisdom, compassion, and rich menu of possibilities.

SUSANNAH SHEFFER

PREFACE TO THE NEW EDITION

What do I want to do when I grow up? For many people that child-hood question persists throughout life. At five it can lead to wild fantasies and lifelong dreams. When remembered and reconsidered in adolescence it has the urgency of budding independence. And in middle age, it has the sadness of an incomplete life. Yet the question persists as long as the imagination is alive. What, of all the possible things that people do, would I love to do? And how do I figure that out? Providing specific ways to help people answer these questions for themselves is the purpose of *The Question is College*, the original working title for which was *Lessons for Life*.

Even though I lost the battle for that title I still believe that is the main point of the book, which I was asked to write by a friend who saw a need to help young people who did not want to go to college figure out sensible alternatives. The book is focused on high school-age youngsters and provides specific ways to go about dis-covering interests, affinities, desires; I quickly learned that it is suit-able for people of all age. When the book was still in manuscript form I gave it to a friend to try out with his teenage daughter. A week later I called and asked how she responded. He told me that she hadn't looked at it since he decided to test out the material on himself and got completely absorbed in his own quest for meaning-ful work. He even suggested that I redo the manuscript so that its audience was broader than the original intent. The question for him was not whether to go to college but how to define a vocation and then worry about whether college or other learning experiences would be useful.

It was too late to change the focus of the book but reviewers pointed out the same thing as he did. In fact, using the book might be a family affair. I received a few letters after the book was pub-lished that described how the profiles and exercises in the book were used as family activities. The most dramatic case I remember was from a high school student who wrote that she, her ten-year-old brother, her mother, and her father went through the book together, then filled in their own profiles and did their own research, and shared the results. She commented that she never realized how much you can learn about someone from their dreams about work, nor had she imagined that work could be more than what you did to make money so you could afford to do what you cared about. Her revelations were at the heart of what I hoped to do with the book—help young people discover that work and vocation are not separated from but an integral part of centered, holistic living.

Finding nurturing work that will also support a modest and decent life is a major challenge in our society. However, rewarding work and modest living are necessities if we are to survive as a nation. Yet the pressure of schooling, the incessant demands that people shape themselves to the technological and corporate demands of the privileged, and the temptations to make and consume more and more get in the way of living a full life that does not elevate greed and self-indulgence to sacred status.

This book stands against those corporate values and can be used as a handbook and guide for seekers of life's work. It takes some translation if you are not in high school or if you are set on going to college. However, it is useful for current college students who have to face the same question of work upon graduation as they did in high school. It is also useful for people thinking about changing jobs, retiring and seeking a way to learn a new vocation or to use the skills acquired over life in different ways.

I remember one of my children's college graduations. We were having dinner after the ceremony and at the end of the meal about a half dozen new graduates began to reflect upon their future. One of them said, "Here we go again," and I asked him what it meant. He said it was just like the end of high school. He had gone through the institution, done well, and was faced, once again, with the question of what to do with his life. The others agreed and I thought of a friend who had just been downsized and was worried about the same thing. The question is not college, but how to build a meaningful life, which is not easy given the pressures to compete, conform, and just get a job.

About eight years ago I was invited to talk to a group of school and adult counselors who had begun to use *The Question is College* in their consultations. They indicated that stress, anxiety, and moderate depression can be relieved by the search for meaningful work and the development of the courage to do what you care to do. Many of their clients found that the daily round of their jobs and the pressures of competing within the framework of dehumanized corporations were as much a cause of neurosis as personal problems and that the techniques provided in the book were useful to their patients.

People are intelligent and sensitive enough to make important decisions for themselves when provided with a little help. It is useful for all of us to spend time taking an inventory of personal strengths and passionate desires, of dreams and values, and making a way to transform this material into a plan for a life's work. This book provides tools that can help in these explorations and plans.

HERBERT KOHL

THE
QUESTION
IS COLLEGE

1

Several Myths About the Virtues of a College Education

LAST YEAR I received a copy of my Harvard College Class of 1958 Anniversary Report and decided that, after thirty years away from Harvard, it was worth reading all 1,400 entries. The report was particularly interesting to me as we had all just reached or passed the age of fifty and had concerns that were quite different than those we had in college. Fifty is a metaphysical age, a time to reflect on work and values, and think about what we have done and what's left to do. Except for those of us who expect to live to one hundred, being fifty implies that more than half of one's life is over. For most of us it is also the time when our children are growing up and leaving home, when our own parents are aging or have passed away, and when major decisions are made that sometimes lead to new careers, divorce, or second families.

All of these concerns are reflected in my classmates' comments. Also, a surprising number of people talked about the need for social and economic justice and for the renewal of the spirit of the civil rights movement, which was part of our coming of age. There was considerable nostalgia for the romance of being part of a social movement and feeling that one was contributing to something larger than oneself.

Many of my classmates also described their children. Of course, there were a number of people whose children went to Harvard and other elite colleges. But a substantial number of my classmates had children who went to smaller colleges or didn't go to college at all. The youngsters who didn't go to college ranged from chefs to musicians, artists, woodworkers, mechanics, environmental activists, community workers, and members of the military, and their fathers seemed to be proud of them. A number of people indicated that they had discovered, with their own children, that college might not be the only route to a full, rewarding adult life.

This intrigued me because I've been working with many young people who have chosen routes to lifetime vocations that do not involve going to college right after high school. These youngsters are not dropouts, or school problems. In fact, most of them are at or near the top of their classes, are engaged in extracurricular activities such as the student council, the school paper, and the band. Some are athletes, and others are involved in art, music, dance, or computer science. These young people decided not to go straight to college after high school, but to work or travel instead, and consider college only if it fit into the larger scheme of what they wanted to do with their lives. They decided to take the time to search for what they wanted to do with their lives and how they wanted to live and work. They refused to rush off to college or center their lives around preparing for well-paying, high-status jobs. In fact, money and status were less important to them than the quality of their lives and the usefulness of the work they did. Many of these young-sters were accused, by their parents and teachers, of being romantic and unrealistic, of not knowing how hard and difficult survival is in our society. Yet it's possible that they are more realistic and sensible than youngsters who force themselves through college in order to prepare themselves to "go out into the world" ready to compete, make money, and wait until retirement to enjoy themselves. There are many good reasons to encourage young people to live modest, socially useful, and personally rewarding lives and avoid the neuroticism and vio-lence that accompanies a single-minded quest for money and status.

Over the past twenty years, watching my children, their friends, and my former students grow, I have changed my own attitudes toward the relationship of vocation to college, and spent a lot of time thinking about what constitutes a satisfying and useful adult life. Going to college has assumed mythic and moral proportions in our society. Getting into a "good" college is considered a sign of superiority and failing to get into one a cause for family shame. Putting money aside for college is con-sidered a major investment for one's child's future. Not having enough money to send a child to college is enough to cause people to take second jobs, work overtime, borrow money, forgo vacations.

In addition, college is supposed to be the place where one acquires the skills needed to succeed in society, the place where one also becomes a well-educated, cultivated person, an individual who knows how to serve the national interest, and a decent citizen. These four so-called virtues are used to sell the importance of a college education for all young people in our society. They merit a bit of analysis.

Let's start with success. If success is measured by income, the things that lead to success are wealthy parents, good con-nections, a certain amount of ruthlessness and daring, luck, and in some cases ingenuity at inventing or trading. Inherited wealth doesn't come from college, though influential connec-tions might be made there. Ruthlessness and daring can be honed at college but are just as easily developed on the streets. College can, however, help one become a sophisticated trader or inventor, though there are other routes to the same skills, as witness the number of developers and entrepreneurs in the computer industry who taught themselves and bypassed college altogether.

Monetary success is not directly related to a college degree, either, though certainly there are some jobs that are tied to credentials and some economic values that come from meeting the right people in college. There are many high school dropouts on the Fortune 500 list, and most major family fortunes were initially made by people who never spent a day at college. Among them are Charles Goodyear, Henry Ford, William C. Durant (founder of General Motors), George Eastman (Eastman Kodak), Marshall Field, Julius Rosenwald (Sears, Roebuck), and John D. Rockefeller. Their children did go to college in many cases, but that was after the family fortune was made, and was as often a route to social respectability as to intellectual and cultural achievement.

If success is measured by rewarding work, college can be useful for youngsters with a direction and passion for some college-related vocation such as the sciences, engineering, archaeology, the study of literature, and the arts. Yet for writers, musicians, mechanics, journalists, computer programmers, and many others, learning through apprenticeship and work in the field is at least as useful as formal schooling.

There are many routes to success and college is only one of them, despite the myth that college equals success and the correlated myth that you know more and have a better chance to succeed if you go to college than if you don't. Success is perhaps more a function of motivation and talent than years in school.

This leads to a second question: "Do students emerge from college as well-educated and cultivated people?" Well, some do. Most probably end up knowing more about football and fraternities than about the arts, history, and other cultural issues. And, given the tension created by exams and rankings, and the overriding power of the myth that you go to college in order to

·

succeed after you leave college, there is little time to form intelligently reasoned opinions, digest the classics, develop critical thinking skills, and in general become well educated. Most college students rush to get through the required courses, as well as their major subject requirements. Their goal is to get out of college and into the world of work, not to deepen knowledge. Some students, of course, take advantage of the possibility of becoming well educated and well informed, but it's not uncommon to meet college graduates whose knowledge and interests are limited to what will help them make money. The tension between going to college to acquire skills for success and going to become well educated has never been resolved. My guess, however, is that most youngsters fall on the success side.

In addition, education to serve the national interest, something much talked about these days, is a fool's game. The national interest cannot be defined with any clarity. One day it is to compete with the Japanese in technology, another to compete with the Russians in the basic sciences, yet another to maintain Western Civilization's cultural dominance over the cultures of our own ethnic minorities. National interest also can mean corporate interest, or the interests of the dominant political ideology. What any of these has to do with a college education isn't clear, unless going to college means being channeled into certain fields or learning to look at the world in an accepted way. And neither of these has to do with producing well-educated, independent-thinking, creative individuals.

As for the relationship between college and decency, one need only think of the number of degrees from the most elitist institutions of higher education in our country held by the architects of the Vietnam war, the destabilization of Chile, and the attempt by the United States to maintain world dominance no matter what means are employed. There are decent credentialed and learned people and indecent ones. And the same holds for people without college experience. Graduating college is no more a guarantee of decency than is belonging to a particular church or coming from a particular ethnic background.

·

7

Is College Always
a Wise
Investment?

THERE ARE valuable things that can be learned at colleges, both culturally and technically, and professions that can only be learned there. For some people college can open up unimagined possibilities and change the whole nature and direction of their lives. However, this isn't true for everyone, and one ought to consider what other useful things there are for young people to do right after high school. For many students, college is just an extension of high school that has virtues that are more social than intellectual or vocational. Going to college means leaving home and having the opportunity of experimenting with independence without the obligation of working full-time to support oneself. College also provides the opportunity to make decisions without parental pressure. College becomes a time in limbo, a time to be away from home and yet not in the world. It is a peer-driven culture, which professors have to fight in order to get students to take learning seriously.

Within that world there are some students who are deeply engaged with their studies, but they are the blessed exceptions that keep professors alive and active in a world in which serious learning is often secondary.

The importance of college from the perspective of the quality of a whole life is vastly overrated. Sending children to college directly after high school may be an expensive and unwise investment if they do not have the slightest idea of what they want to make of their lives. Sometimes youngsters realize this and refuse to allow their parents to invest in their college education. Several young people I know, appreciating the financial burden their parents would have to bear to send them to college, refused to go. Two of them got jobs and the third went into the military. They told their parents that they weren't opposed to college per se but needed to discover what they wanted to do first. They respected their parents' willingness to make sacrifices but didn't want the sacrifices to be for nothing. All three of them had friends who had graduated college and had no idea what they wanted to do with their lives and had no use for the degrees they had obtained.

Colleges do not provide the experience or the breadth of vision that allow young people to get a feel for what they might love to do with their lives. In fact, for many youngsters college is a distraction, a delaying tactic, a way of putting off deciding upon a life's work for another four years after high school. Unfortunately, that delay can become extended throughout life, and many people live either without having discovered what they would like to make their life's work or discover it too late to do it.

I remember talking to the writer and educator John Holt several years before he died. He had found toward the end of his life what he wished would have been his life's work: playing

.

9

the cello. When he was over forty-five he began cello lessons and wrote, in *It's Never Too Late,* about how he discovered this vocation and pursued it despite all of the other things he was supposed to be doing. I mention this because of the transformation I saw in John as he followed his vocation and passion. He told me that the courage to take up the cello when he was supposed to be too old to learn to play well was one of the most important steps in his life. He said he wished that everyone would have the courage, earlier in life, to follow their inner urges toward vocation and not let some silly sense of the proper way to be schooled interfere with their learning and degrade the quality of their lives.

The exploration of vocational choice—that is, the opportunity to discover what meaningful and rewarding work can occupy a lifetime—is too often delayed until after college, after getting a job, after having a family . . . after too much living. Mid-life crisis, angst when one's children leave home, depression created by meaningless work (however financially rewarding) and a sense of having achieved nothing with one's life are not uncommon experiences in our culture. Nor is it uncommon to believe that college will somehow make it possible for our children to escape our own frustrations.

The idea that one has to go to college directly after high school, or that once in college one has to stay for four consecutive years without taking a break, has to be rethought. *A full life is more important than a college degree, and discovering and doing what one wants to do is more important than having credentials or making a lot of money.*

College is an expensive investment of time and money, and should be made cautiously and with purpose. It may be more sensible for young people to spend time discovering a personal focus and *then* to decide whether to attend or bypass college.

· · · · · · · · · · · · · · · · · · · **3** · · ·

The
Changing Face
of
College

"YOU HAVE to go to college to get a good job."

This is preached to every high school student in the United States, whether or not they have the slightest interest in anything that might be learned in college. It is almost a threat, which implies that if you don't go to college, you won't get a good job or even be able to lead a good life. College is supposed to provide a passport to prosperity and security, and to validate the quality of a person. College is not identified with learning so much as with credentials for future employment.

However, a college degree only certifies four years of passage from home to work. It doesn't imply anything about skills, talents, experiences, or qualifications. It is a piece of paper that says you took the next step after high school and shows that you have the patience to delay entry into the world of work for four years and have demonstrated the ability to continue to do what your teachers want you to do. Consequently, college degrees, especially those in nontechnical subjects, provide minimal guarantees that someone might be a reliable and obedient worker.

It's not clear that college is the only road to jobs or success. There are many successful people who didn't go to college and many decent jobs that do not require college degrees. The entertainment industry, which in the United States employs more people and makes more money than either the steel or fishing industry, is full of musicians, producers, technicians, actors, dancers, and others who did not go to college. Many computer hackers produce first-rate software while they're still in high school and learn through hackers' networks, often in pizza parlors and not in classrooms. In addition, there are many people in small businesses, ranging from bakeries to restaurants, from small publishing houses and print shops to doll and stained-glass makers to fine furniture workers and clothes designers, who learned their skills on the job and through informal exchange with other people in their fields. The total number of people who provide these services is large; it is estimated that over 10 percent of the working population in San Francisco, for example, is involved in crafts or the arts.

The tradition of expecting young people to attend college before entering the workplace is no more than forty years old, dating from the end of the Second World War, when the GI Bill subsidized college education for returning veterans. The affluence that followed the Second World War gave a lot of people a sense of upward social mobility, and college became the ticket to respectability. This often had little to do with what one actually *learned* in college. Moreover, many of the people who attended college after the war were older and had a clearer sense of how they wanted to spend their lives. I think that this clarity based on experience is lacking in most recent high school graduates. The rush to college often makes college an extension of high school and an opportunity to delay thinking about one's life work. I think it would be wise for parents not to worry so much about what college their children will get into and instead spend time helping youngsters examine the quality of different forms of work and different ways of living.

If you care about your children's whole life, not just their college career, you have to think beyond college before you even think about what college they might get into. The quest for vocation, the search for getting the skills to do satisfying work over a lifetime, has to be separated from the game of getting into a "good" college. This often requires rethinking one's own priorities, of backing away from the foolish propaganda about the importance of a college education, and looking closely, and with love, into the hearts of your children. It is essential that those of us whose parents sacrificed to allow us to go to college realize that our children do not live in the same social, economic, or emotional world that characterized our parents' lives.

My grandmothers and grandfathers did not have any formal schooling. Their dream was for their children to go to college. Neither my mother nor her sisters and brothers made it. They all dropped out of high school because of economic necessity. They had to work to support the family. On my father's side, my dad and his youngest brother went to college. His sisters and another brother didn't. They learned the realities of hard work very early in life. In fact, my father, now, more than fifty years after his graduation, still talks about how wonderful it was for him to have had the opportunity to attend college and makes sure to give a generous donation to his alma mater each year. For him college was a gift, a road toward a fuller, less difficult life.

Now comes my generation. All of the adults in my parents' generation insisted, wanted, and needed their children to go to college and were willing to make personal sacrifices to see it happen. College meant jobs, status, and respectability. It meant a less harsh and more protected life than they had experienced. As they moved into the middle class they accepted the myth that if your children did not go to college it was a discredit to you and a cause for serious worry about your children's future.

·

1 3

They lived with the constant fear of poverty created by having grown up in the Depression and hoped that, somehow, by having credentials or becoming professionals, their children would have some protection against another such horror.

I remember a neighbor across the street from me in the Bronx during the early 1950s, the mother of one of my friends, who showed me her bankbooks and the cans of food she had piled up in the closets. She told me the cans were in case the Depression came again. At least her family would be able to eat. The bankbooks were to send her children to college so they would be protected by their degrees.

If your children did go to college, even if they didn't use what they learned, or didn't acquire any specific skills, you had done your job as parents. You had given them the gift of college. That was from the late 1940s to the mid-1960s.

For the most part, my parents and their brothers, sisters, and friends succeeded in putting their children through college. My brother and sister and I, my cousins, and most of my friends, with the exception of two who are now millionaires, went to college. Some have turned out well, some not so well. The extended family we knew as children has disappeared as people moved off to the suburbs, leaving the old people behind. There are many single-parent families in my generation; a number of people are searching for new careers in midlife, and some feel that the rewards they were promised when they went off to college were simply not worth the pain. Very few of us do work that is directly related to what we learned at college. I'm a writer and schoolteacher, and studied mathematics and philosophy at college. These studies have made my work and life rich, but I did not learn to teach or write at college.

However, college did mean, for members of my generation, a way into a world larger than the one we grew up in. It meant meeting people and encountering ideas and artistic and cultural expressions that were simply not available at home.

And many of us are closer to our children, more involved in their lives, than our parents had time to be. We have benefited from a more secure existence, from the connections we made at college, from the skills we acquired there, and from our greater mobility within society.

We now have children who have reached college age. We were different from our parents, and our children are different from us. Some of the differences can be attributed to our lives. We've been able to offer our children what our parents couldn't offer them: the cultural and class perspectives of people who have graduated from college, and our experiences in the civil rights, antiwar, and environmental movements and in careers that were unthinkable and unavailable to our parents.

However, we have not been able to offer them, in an adequate way, the coherence and camaraderie of working-class society, or the funniness and casual social world of crowded urban communities where people had common cultures and values. We are mobile like most Americans. My wife is from Cleveland, I'm from the Bronx, and we now live in rural northern California. When I talk to my children about my own life in the Bronx they find it fascinating and interesting but are so far from the feeling and smell of it that it frustrates me in a way I imagine my grandfather was frustrated explaining to me and my cousins what it was like to be growing up a Jew in the Pale between 1885 and 1904.

The gap between the world of my generation's children and the world we adults experience is intensified by our vulnerability and the wounds we have suffered trying to make it in society. Over the past twenty years, divorce and single-parent families have become common, sexuality has become more casual, and friendships and relationships have seemed more troubled. Economic and social tension is ordinary, as is substance abuse. People in my generation accept with a casualness bordering on mild compassion the idea that every one of their friends is hurting in some way, either at work or in personal or social life. We are part of what might be called a generation of the walking wounded, surviving as best we can the pressures of a competitive society at war with itself and, as Vietnam, Nicaragua, Grenada, Libya, and the Middle East illustrate, the world.

And our children know of our hurts and our foibles without

our having to tell them. I have often felt that our children are growing up wiser than we did and are prematurely adult. They have experienced, either directly or indirectly, divorce, violence, adult substance abuse, and adult stress. These pains of adult life are common knowledge to our children whether they have experienced them within their own families or in the families of friends, and they become the children's pains. I have talked to many children, some as young as seven and eight, and they are more psychologically sophisticated and sensitive than most adults I know. It is not because they are young and look at the world with innocent and open eyes. Rather it is that they have experienced too much too soon. This applies as much to middle-class and upper-class children as it does to the children of the poor.

In my past ten years of teaching, well over half of my students witnessed a divorce in the family, and a large number of them live in single-parent families. (Incidentally, the highest percentage of these children came from middle-class families whose parents had college degrees.) They were, almost without exception, accustomed to sorrow.

Marriage and love are not the same as they were in my parents' and grandparents' generations. My grandparents, for example, were betrothed by arrangement and met only once or twice before they were married. They did not have a choice. My parents had a choice, but economics was as much a pressure as love in their lives, and it would never have occurred to them that there was a choice to unmarry. Yet in my generation, stable two-parent families seem like dinosaurs, something kids study in the early grades of school and see occasionally in homes that may seem to them like museum settings. Young people are more sensitive to personal relations, know more psychology, are more cynical about adults, and have a greater sense of being in a worldwide youth culture than my peers and I did when I was growing up.

Things that were unthinkable to us are ordinary to them. They have grown up in a world in which the theory of relativity, black holes, and microchips are ordinary. Recently I tried to teach something about Freud to a number of high school students, and I remember that when we read some of his comments on penis envy, all of the students, females and males, said that this guy must have had some problem. Freud was ordinary and funny, a troubled man who needed, as one of the students said, to read modern psychological theory and Buddhism. When I was growing up, Freud was treated as slightly dangerous but perhaps correct in his analysis of sexuality.

In addition, our children, and a substantial number of other American youths, are heirs to an electronic and international community, however loosely defined. They are part of a cross-cultural-youth social world that defines itself through style, music, the visual arts, dance, and language. They are not afraid of the Russians, are horrified and confused by the cruelty in South Africa, and don't understand how segregation could have been part of our culture.

Thirty years ago there was no youth music industry. We listened to the same music our parents did. There was no line of clothes for adolescents, no radio or TV programmed to attract the teen market. There was no national attention given to runaways and perhaps there weren't as many youngsters deciding to leave home. Nor was there such widespread concern about young people who, in one way or another, resist adult control.

And many young people, themselves, are cynical about adults' ability to create a decent world. They worry and dream about the possibility of a nuclear war that could make a life's work meaningless in a few seconds. They are burdened with having inherited a world out of control and, on a more personal level, parents barely in control of their own lives. They see adults, college-educated adults, who often seem no more capable of coherent and meaningful lives than eleventh or twelfth graders. I can't count the number of times I've heard teenagers comment on how badly older people have messed up the world and their own lives.

The teenagers I'm talking about tend to have their own rooms, their own stereos and record collections. They, like my own children, have not grown up in poverty and have not directly experienced hunger or extreme violence. They are taken care of, and if they work during high school it is not for survival but for extra cash. Their parents love them, though they often take out their own frustrations on them. Many of these youngsters see the world, outside of home and a small group of friends, as a threat. They know about violence, drugs, war, AIDS; about the consequences of trying to survive in a competitive and cruel world even when you have money.

One high school senior said to me recently, when I asked him what he and his friends wanted to do with their lives, "All we want to do is play our music and skateboard to paradise." Another summarized the situation this way: "Why go to college and grow up and get a good job if all that'll happen to you is that you'll end up like the people who call themselves adults?"

The strength of youth culture, which I believe is a dominant aspect of our current cultural life, comes from their often stylish rejection and defiance of the respectable adult world. It is also hopeful and positive. We have educated our children to know more than we do and sometimes they point out, in uncomfortable ways, how we adults have misvalued what is truly of value. A college degree is one of the misvalued things that has to be reconsidered. There are more important things to consider for many adolescents than whether or not they get into a good college.

It is for us, the parents, to learn what these things are, to try to understand the world as young people experience it.

Most of the adults I know, whether they are investment bankers or social radicals who want to transform the world, have college degrees. Our children have grown up in a world where having a college degree is ordinary, not special. For them college is less of a concern than is life. They are worried about doing something that will be interesting and at the same time useful. For them, unless college is seen as more than a reward for suffering through high school or as an extension of adolescence, there are many compelling reasons not to go.

And, as far as I am concerned, there is no reason for someone's going on to college if there is nothing she or he wants to learn there. On the contrary, college can be an expensive waste of time—or worse, a time when many young people learn how to cultivate selfishness, celebrate violence, separate

.
1 8

work and pleasure, develop cynical attitudes toward the value and beauty of learning, and practice, in groups of their peers, all of the prejudices that our society has struggled to eliminate. One need only think about sports and party mania, the volume of business done by crib note companies, the resurgence of racism on many campuses, and fraternity and sorority arrogance and irresponsibility to get a picture of many colleges as glorified singles bars and business clubs rather than places of learning. In that sense, sadly, these students may indeed be training for life in our society.

4

Going
to College:
Making
the Question
Personal

THERE ARE many strategies for working with young people and deciding, with them, whether college is appropriate. There is a danger in forcing young people into college, or in rejecting them if they drop out or refuse to go. The resentment that such attitudes can create may color the whole future relationship you have with your children. In my experience, lasting and loving family relationships develop when young people are supported even though they resist your dreams for them and decide to do something on their own. There is as much delicacy and compassion required in dealing with post–high school decisions as there is in nurturing an infant.

Robert, a young man I've known since he was four or five, graduated from high school five years ago. He had a hard passage and felt that he would rather clean motel rooms than spend another year at anything that resembled a school. His parents, both of whom have college degrees, felt it would be a disgrace to the family and a sign to the neighbors that they weren't good parents, if Robert spent the year after high school making less than five dollars an hour rather than going to college. In my judgment, Robert genuinely needed a rest and some time to sort out his desires and aspirations. However, his parents couldn't bear the thought of their son doing menial work while most of his friends were in college, and so family life became hell in the last months before graduation. Robert deliberately did terribly on the SAT exam and wrote the worst essays he could dream of on the college applications that were forced down his throat. He made sure no college would accept him, and none did. His parents were angry, embarrassed, dismayed. One night they threatened to throw him out of the house after he graduated and make him support himself if he didn't go to junior college at least. He told me it was a delight to hear that because they were telling him to do just what he intended to do anyway.

After graduating high school Robert got a job at a gas station, not a motel, and rented an apartment with some friends. Now, five years later, he's the manager of a shoe store, married, and totally unwilling to see his parents or let them see his daughter. He's also enrolled at the local junior college and studying business management. His life is not bad, but the sorrow of his relationship with his parents hangs over all of their lives.

A completely different thing happened to two other young people I've known, James and Alicia. They also had hard passages through high school, and also refused to play the game of going on to college. There was simply nothing there they wanted to learn, and they wanted to do, as James said, "real work in the real world." For him, high school was not the real world but some kind of dream (he actually said "nightmare") you walked through while you waited for the summers. His parents were sympathetic. They gave him as much support as they could to get him through high school, but realized there was no way of pushing him into college. In fact, they went out of their way to introduce him to friends of theirs who might provide some kind of job while he sorted out what he wanted to do with his life. He worked for a year as a receptionist in a veterinarian's office, and though he didn't particularly like the job, he enjoyed earning money on his own and having freedom and independence. Now he's decided to become a bartender, and though his parents are professionals, they are still supportive. "After all," his father told me, "life hardly ends at twenty-one, and besides, we want to be close to him when we're really old." These days James is flirting with the idea of opening a video rental shop. He loves films and always helps his friends select videos to rent. His mother and father feel it's a good idea, something stable and directly related to a long-term interest of his. They offered to loan him money to open a shop if he puts up part of the capital and he is seriously considering taking the plunge.

James's parents don't feel he would be embarrassing the family by running a shop. They have a genuine concern for him, not for what he looks like to neighbors, and as a consequence their house has become a gathering place for James's friends. They feel comfortable in James's house because they know they are respected there for who they are and will not be put down for failing to conform to some societal image of the success-bound youngster.

Alicia also refused college and went to work nights in a home for severely retarded children. Her role was essentially custodial and she earned the minimum wage. Her mother and father told me that their dream was for her to become a doctor and they were disappointed she didn't get on with her education, because going to medical school takes such a long time. They had long and sometimes bitter arguments with Alicia over college. They also had sessions with Alicia's guidance counselor, who agreed with them that she should go directly to college after high school. She felt that there was a conspiracy against her and once told her parents that she simply was going to move out if they didn't get off her back.

There was something in the strength of her statement that caused her parents to retreat. They didn't want to be rejected by her: Parents fear rejection as much as children do. They took the advice of their hearts more seriously than the advice of the high school counselor and found ways to think positively about Alicia's work.

At this time Alicia is still working at the home. She has been promoted to the day shift and trained to run education programs. She's taking some classes in psychology and art therapy at the local junior college. Recently she expressed a tentative desire to get a psychology degree and open her own home with county funding. And she and her parents have never been closer.

While I was writing this section, two of my former high school students, now both thirty-three, came by to visit. Chris and Julie never finished high school. Chris is now ranked among the twenty-five top nineball pool players in the United States and Julie's a member of Actor's Equity and has worked with Sam Shepard and Peter Coyote at the Magic Theater in San Francisco. They told me that their lives have not been easy but they are getting happier and stronger over the years and couldn't imagine doing anything else. Thinking about their lives, I realized how easy it is to forget how many different ways there are to live full ones.

When he was still in high school, Chris told me that he was going to be a professional pool player. I considered it a whim, an adolescent dream. However, he recently told me that when he split from school after lunch he went to the pool halls and was being taught the game by the best players in the Bay Area. He loved the world of professional pool: To him it was fun and also dignified and rewarding work, as acting was to Julie. He didn't care about what other people thought about his obsession.

It is very important—for all of us—to refuse to be trapped

into society's stereotypes or to listen to the advice of its agents. Everyone can find a place for herself or himself if allowed the time to explore the possibilities and if there is access to decent and loving advice. There are some high school guidance counselors who can also be helpful, but in my experience the advice that comes from the high school usually depends upon school performance rather than an intimate knowledge of young people's dreams and aspirations. "Good" students are channeled in one way, "bad" ones in others. A student who gets Cs and wants to be a doctor is channeled into nursing or ambulance driving, but an A student who wants to be a park ranger or paramedic is channeled into an undergraduate premedical program.

The fact is, school counseling is usually cold and mechanical. Students are rarely encouraged to try things that their grades don't seem to qualify them for. Yet motivation often counts for more than grades, and young people who have a direction, and have some support, can usually get where they want to go with or without good grades. The problem is that often high school counselors are a burdened species. There are usually too few of them at a school to spend time knowing the individual needs and aspirations of all the students. Budget cutbacks have reduced their ability to be effective, and it is very easy for them to fall into the habit of playing favorites and measuring their effectiveness by the college admissions they can achieve and the cash value of the scholarships they can muster rather than by the quality of their advice. Too often they are not student advocates so much as gatekeepers, letting some students in and keeping others out of the institutions they judge appropriate. However, the rare counselor who cares is like a member of the family, and should be part of the student's support network as early as possible in his or her high school career.

5

Exploring
the
Options

IT'S HARD for many parents to think of their children as departing from the usual route taken from adolescence to adulthood through college. There are many things that get in the way of clear and sensible thinking when it comes to one's children's future. Promises of future success and happiness figure prominently in the way "experts" tell uncertain parents to deal with their children. Predictions about what will be useful for a young person to do with her or his life come from politicians, pollsters, and media people for whom some new trend makes a good story.

These days parents are uncertain and youngsters are confused—with good reason. Who can be sure that a career in
computer programming will be any more secure ten years from
now than being a musician, or that an MBA will have any more
security than someone cooking in a gourmet restaurant? Today,
teachers and social workers earn less than taxicab drivers and
factory workers.

Just think of the recent stock market crash and imagine the
future ones. The economic stability of our society is very ten-
uous, and it's impossible to tell what will happen over the next
five years. What will be better then, an M.B.A. degree from
Stanford or a taxi medallion in New York City, when considered
from the perspective of a whole life? Whose life will be fuller,
a corporate executive's or a second violinist's in the Cleveland
Orchestra?

These questions are both personal and social: The value of
credentials changes with changing economic conditions, and
without an intrinsic reason to follow a career, there is always
the danger of finding adult life shallow and meaningless. This
isn't a frivolous matter when you try to give advice to high
school–aged children.

I remember about ten years ago there was a campaign in
schools throughout the country to entice young people into
computer programming as the road to a good job and, by implication, a posh life. Now, in the Bay Area, there aren't many jobs
for the youngsters who bit the bait, and it's quite common to
meet a programmer driving a cab or tending bar. One young
programmer even told me that I should advise all my students
to get a bartender's license before they get an M.S. in computer
science.

Uncertainty characterizes our society. There are very few
secure jobs, no industry that is free from raiding or removal to
some other country, no sure way to a decent life, and many
young people, about to leave high school, are aware of that.
They are much more concerned about creating a life they can
control than accepting the uncertain promises of imagined
success.

It is probably best to think about your child's future from

the point of view of what the philosopher Spinoza called *sub speciae eternitatus*—that is, from the aspect of eternity. It means looking at the present from the perspective of the future, of the end of one's life, and not making decisions that simply relate to tomorrow or even the next four years. Think your way on to the future. We'll all be old and our children will have children and in the end the closeness we have to each other is more important than becoming a doctor, lawyer, or millionaire.

Questions about life after high school work their way into the heart of a family. Over the past five years they have certainly occupied our family as our three children prepared to graduate from high school, graduated, and made choices about what they would like to do with their lives. I worried that if the wrong decision were made they would suffer. I now feel that my notion of life after high school was inappropriate and realize how much more there is to do in the world than taking the secure way of delaying life for four years in a "regular" college.

My oldest child, Tonia, who did quite well in high school, informed us a few months before her graduation that she wasn't going to attend school the next year. It upset me but didn't surprise me. High school had been boring and barely tolerable for her. She didn't want another year of feeling that she hadn't grown or learned much that was of use to her. This feeling, I think, was heightened by the hysteria and anxiety of taking SATs, filling out college application forms, worrying about grade point averages, and, consequently, not having had adequate time to explore in depth what she might like to do with her life.

She didn't go straight to college but wanted to get a sense of whether painting and drawing was a possible vocation for her. She didn't know whether she was good enough to pursue an artistic career and had had no time in high school to spend hours drawing and painting, and probably wouldn't at the colleges she could get into. She needed that year after high school to explore what she might be able to do and so, instead of going to college, went to art school part-time.

Tonia also did volunteer work for the newsletter of an antinuclear group and became involved with a whole new group of friends, many of whom were several years older than she was. After that year she took the plunge and became a full-time art student and is now a senior. The year off gave her a control of her life and a confidence about herself as an artist that I doubt she would have gotten if she had gone off to college full-time and managed to fit in an art class or two. Recently she graduated from art college.

My daughter Erica, who is a junior in college, is taking her junior year off to do community work. Her desire is to be in the world of work and not go through four years of college without testing herself in a larger world where she has social and work responsibilities. It took me a while to adjust to her decision. I was uncertain about her choice at first, but I've come to realize that she's right to test out the usefulness of what she's learning in a work situation.

Erica's choice reminded me of something Ben Shahn, the painter, said in a lecture that I attended during college, on the education of an artist:

> Attend a university if you possibly can. There is no content of knowledge that is not pertinent to the work you will want to do. But before you attend a university work at something for a while. Do anything. Get a job in a potato field; or work as a grease monkey in an auto repair shop. But if you do work in a field do not fail to observe the look and feel of the earth and of the things that you handle—yes, even the potatoes! Or in the auto shop the smell of oil and grease and burning rubber. . . . Listen well to all conversations and be instructed by them, and take all seriousness seriously. Never look down upon anything or anyone as not worthy of notice. In college or out of college, read. And form opinions! . . . Never be afraid to become embroiled in art or life or politics.

One interesting implication of Shahn's quote is that young people need to find ways of breaking out of youth culture in order to broaden their experience. They should know their parents' friends, be part of "grown-up" parties and dinners and other social occasions. They should visit their parents and their parents' friends at work. It is very important for your children to know your friends and be able to turn to them for advice and perhaps even inspiration. It's also important for high school students to get out of the classroom and see what goes on in the many worlds of work that might be possible for them.

I've found myself talking a lot with parents of high school students about the anxiety we all feel about our children's decisions, about our fear that our children might fall behind or get lost or hurt by not taking the easy way. Even though we acknowledge that there really is no easy way to a decent life, and that living in consonance with one's inner needs and social commitments is essential, we worry about our children's future and admire their courage at the same time.

It's hard for our children to understand how we worry about them. I think that's particularly true during the years they are in high school and right after they graduate. There's a lot to worry about that youngsters don't find such a big deal. Driving a car is one source of anxiety; drugs and sex are others. Thoughts of these dangers can lead to sleepless nights, family quarrels, alienation. So long as your children are still living at home, no matter how trustworthy they are, you wait to hear them come in at night. Probably they're with friends and not thinking about you and your anxiety at all. We've had to convince our children that we worried about them even when, from their point of view, there was nothing to worry about, and arrange for them to call whenever they changed plans. Most of the time they did.

If it's hard for youngsters to understand their parents' specific everyday anxieties, it is even more difficult for them to comprehend the way parents can worry about their children's future. And it's natural to want the passage into adulthood to be easy for our children, to want to smooth the way for them. And going to college seems an easier route than years of experimentation in the world, free of institutional ties.

Such a route isn't easy, but neither is college. Parental anxiety about the daily life of a child who hasn't gone to college is surprisingly the same as it is about a child who has gone. It would be awful not to worry and foolish to worry too much.

The
Importance
of
Parental
Support

OVER THE past ten years I have seen many young people choose to do work they love that has little or nothing to do with going to college. It is almost as if they have reinvented, for themselves, the notion of the dignity of all work, whether it is manual, commercial, social, intellectual, or artistic, so long as it is chosen and provides inner rewards. They look on college as a resource that is available on their terms and in ways they find useful, and could be called rebels who know how to succeed. They have no trouble reading, have a thousand things they like to do, and have a rich life learning outside of the context of school.

. . . .

One example is Alec, a nephew of mine, who decided to delay going to college for a year. Instead he spent time traveling around Europe for a few months and then worked as a carpenter. During his high school years he had been to Nicaragua with a church group and had been involved in student politics. He's thinking of a career in international development work. At present he's attending Harvard, and when we talked last summer he told me how surprised he was at the confusion about vocation and meaning he found in many of his classmates. He said that working and traveling had given a focus to his life that he could never have achieved going straight to college.

Alec is not the only one who has delayed going to college in order to get a touch of the real world. An article in *U.S. News and World Report* (February 23, 1988) entitled "College? Hey, give me a break" describes a number of youngsters who chose to explore vocational options before going to college. One of them, who managed to get an apprenticeship doing production and public relations at Appalshop, which produces records and films on Appalachian culture, commented, "I wasn't ready for college. A lot of my friends went straight into college and screwed up. I wanted to see what it was like out there first."

The article describes other youngsters who did things as diverse as teaching English at a YMCA in Korea and working as an au pair in Europe and auditing a few classes at universities at the same time.

Roger is another example of a youngster who didn't go straight to college after graduating from high school. Roger's mother has a Ph.D. in biology and his father is a lawyer. His younger sister is a freshman at a prestigious eastern college. He has never had a desire to go to college, and from the time he was young his favorite thing was cooking. His parents worried that he'd never be able to make it as an adult unless he got out of the kitchen.

Senior year in high school was a nightmare. His parents, teachers, and counselors put pressure on him to apply to college. Many of the students made fun of him for wanting to cook, though he did have a small and congenial group of friends who supported and encouraged him. They were called the "loners" by other high school students, and consisted of skateboarders, musicians and artists, and other students who identified themselves as punk or hard rock. They used style to distinguish themselves from the other students at the school and protected and supported each other in ways that the more competitive and conforming students never did. Each one, feeling different, could appreciate how the others felt.

Roger's parents and teachers accused him of being a failure, of not appreciating what they were trying to do for him, of laziness and irresponsibility, and several times he came close to running away from home. He did just manage to graduate.

The summer after graduation he got a job as a dishwasher at a local French restaurant. He told the manager of the restaurant that he wanted to learn how to be a chef. The manager said he was welcome to wash dishes and after a while they'd see if anything else could be worked out.

After a year at the restaurant, Roger worked his way up to assistant dessert chef and then moved to a café where he was breakfast chef and did dishes at night. That was a difficult time for Roger and his parents. He lived at home and knew that his mother and father felt awkward about his not being in college. They were especially ashamed about explaining to their friends what Roger was doing with his life. There were some very tense confrontations. His father, in particular, expressed anger, rage, and shame, and carried on every once in a while about what he had done to have a son like Roger. Then he would swing to the complete opposite position and go out and buy Roger expensive cookbooks and give him catalogs of famous cooking schools, where Roger would be taught by master chefs. That way the shame of having a chef for a son would be alleviated because his son would be a culinary artist, not a mere cook.

Roger's father, Peter, struggled that year with his love for his son and his confusion about the disappointment of his own desires for Roger's future. One particularly painful night he confronted Roger and told him that if he didn't shape up and plan to go to college and get a sensible job the next year he would be disowned and thrown out of the house. Roger's response was that he'd just as soon leave the next day.

Peter realized that Roger wasn't kidding and tried to look at the cause of their mutual misery. What was it: college, dreams of what life would be like in twenty years, anxiety about Roger's future, a lack of trust in Roger's ability to take care of himself? Any of these might destroy their relationship if Roger walked out of the house. It was hard for Peter to back off, and yet he couldn't deal with the thought, which seemed stupid when he thought about it in bed that night, that he was angry at his son for working, for trying to do something he cared about, and for fighting for his independence. He decided to accept Roger's choice of vocation and, the next morning, offered to pay Roger's tuition at cooking school if he wanted to attend. Peter said that the money they had set aside for a college education should be used for Roger's learning whether it was at college or not.

Roger's mother, Ruth, didn't have the same problems with Roger's choice of vocation. She had already set aside some money for Roger and was going to sneak it to him if her husband opposed giving their son the money they had saved for college.

This question of career choice, of cooking instead of college, had become a test of family loyalty and coherence. Fortunately, Roger's father decided to reexamine his priorities and became supportive rather than remaining adamantly opposed to desires he did not understand.

Roger didn't take up his parents' offer of tuition at a cooking school. He said he wasn't ready yet, but might take them up on it sometime. He didn't want to go to chef's school; he wanted to cook and wash dishes and make desserts and spend time in the kitchens of different restaurants. He wanted to know how they worked and how the people who were good chefs functioned. They were his teachers and he felt he needed a few more years in the kitchen with them.

Roger's parents had no idea how much their attitude had injured him and how important their feelings about his work were to him. He wanted to be accepted, respected, and approved of for the person he was, and not for some socially approved educational institution he might attend. He put his parents in a situation where they were forced to reexamine their attitudes, not just toward him, but toward the dignity of different types of work. They had to admit that they felt that investing in chef's school, or any other learning experiences Roger had wanted, was a waste of money, whereas they felt that the outrageous tuition they paid for their daughter's college education was a good investment because of the prestige of the college rather than because of anything she was learning there.

Roger was a bit wary of his parents' sudden conversion but decided to bear with them. There is a time when children become the judges of their parents, when they know things about their parents that the parents have forgotten about themselves. And Roger knew that there would be a lot of hesitancy before his parents fully accepted the fact that he intended to stay in the kitchen all his life.

Roger's example is very important. It is easy to put a dollar value on education and say that a fancy college is worth more than cooking school, that law school is worth more than art school, that medical school is worth more than cabinetmaking school. This way of placing value on work is characteristic of people in my generation in our society. We are the ones who have made it through college and have too often turned away from the value of labor that our grandparents had. Yet often our children see a bigger world, one in which many forms of work lead to dignity and in which the financial rewards of work are less important than the personal and spiritual rewards.

It is important to support the dreams of young people and be with them when they explore what is one of the most essential aspects of their existence: the choice of a vocation. Getting a good job in the hope of doing something satisfying with the money and time one earns by becoming rich is foolish. Becoming rich is a gamble itself, and staying healthy while struggling to succeed is even chancier. A full but modest life dedicated to meaningful work makes more sense.

. . . .

Roger is now doing a chef's tour of Europe, washing dishes in some of the best restaurants and learning how to cook by watching, tasting, and asking intelligent questions. He has said that if he learns enough he may ask his parents to use the money they have put aside for cooking school to set him up in a small restaurant some time in the future.

Roger is trying to discover how to function in a world that intrigues him and these days doesn't visit home much. He doesn't really want his parents' money and tries hard to accept the idea that they'll never fully accept him for the person he wants to be. The harshest statement Roger has ever made about the situation is that he refuses to cook for his parents.

It's interesting that a few weeks after I last talked to Roger I heard a speech given to the Cleveland City Club by Albert Shanker, president of the American Federation of Teachers, that described a similar situation. Shanker said that his son decided to become a cook instead of going to college, and described his own frustration and anxiety at having a child who chose the kitchen instead of the college classroom. To his credit, Shanker spoke in a moving way about how he adjusted to his son's choice rather than destroy their relationship. He also spoke about how the experience changed his thinking about the kind of education and options youngsters should be provided in schools.

Dignified
Life's
Work

KAREN IS another high school graduate who didn't choose college, though she certainly could have, based on her grade point average and SAT scores. Her father is a practicing psychologist. Her mother has a degree in fine arts and is a well-respected painter and weaver. Her younger brother is in college studying business. With the exception of Karen, they are all mild-mannered people who don't easily get upset about anything. This has sometimes been a cause of frustration for Karen.

Karen has a temper. And she has unusually high standards. Throughout her life she has made exacting demands on herself and this has often led to frustration. Getting an A— in school meant failing to get an A. Losing a game of basketball or volleyball meant personal failure, not team failure.

Karen came in third in her high school class with a 3.8 grade point average. Yet as well as she did in high school she never cared for school and swore that the day she got her diploma she was done with school forever. She knew how to fill out forms, which she said was all you ever had to know to get an A or A— in high school. But she didn't like to sit in rooms and did like to choose her own reading. She liked to move and to be outside.

Karen has never minded working; the first job she got when she left high school was repairing bicycles. Getting the job wasn't easy, because she was told it wasn't girl's work and she had to fight to show her competence. However, one of her great pleasures was to go on long bike rides in the country, and she taught herself how to break down and put together her own bike. In addition, she set herself up in a small business in her garage repairing friends' bikes and getting spare parts by cannibalizing abandoned bikes.

Karen moved from bicycles to motorcycles and cars and became a first-rate mechanic. However, she always enjoyed working with wood more than with machines and decided to go to a local vocational training school after high school. Her choice was initially a social embarrassment to her parents, who thought she had made a frivolous decision that was below her skills and beneath their class. She paid no attention to their admonishments that she go to college and do carpentry as a hobby. She told them she had a lot of hobbies and building with wood wasn't one of them. It was work she wanted to do: a vocation, not a leisure enterprise.

Things became so tense at home that Karen moved into an apartment with three of the other students in her carpentry classes. Two of them were male and one was female, and none of them went out with each other. They were friends, though she couldn't convince her parents of that. They didn't realize that, in a way that their and my generation could never have imagined, it is possible for males and females to be friends, share apartments, and not sleep together. We are so far away from our children's worlds sometimes that we need to be reeducated by them. Karen's reeducation project finally succeeded when she brought her boyfriend to dinner at her parents' house. He wasn't one of her roommates, though he was in her carpentry class. Parents still have a hard time adjusting to the fundamental changes in sexual relations that are taking place among many young people, but are aware of the fact that if they want to remain in contact with their children they will have to change their attitudes.

Karen took a job as an apprentice carpenter after graduating from vocational school. Her parents still tried to channel her to college and she paid no attention. She is a sensitive young woman, reads a lot, and has friends who are involved in everything from motorcycle racing to medical school. And she spends time on political activity ranging from protesting apartheid to fighting for the rights of women and young people.

The family situation was quite tense for years because Karen, though she doesn't seek out conflict, doesn't back away from it. And as her life became stable and she became content with the quality of her work, her parents became less important in her life. She respected them but not their attitude toward her, and went out of her way to see them no more than a few times a year. She took little pleasure in their company.

It took a long time for Karen's parents to acknowledge that she was supporting herself, felt pride in her work, and was quite happy—rare things for young people in our society. Still that old nagging sense that she should have "done better with her life" kept coming up during the time they spent together, and turned her into a stranger to them. Their obsession with college and success lost them a child.

Karen did go back to school briefly to get a contractor's license. She now owns a small contracting firm in partnership with her, as she puts it, "significant other" and several of her old friends and they're doing fairly well—that is, well enough for her to live the modest and rewarding life she has carved out for herself. Karen has a child and a family and friends she's proud of, is not starving, feels pride in her work, and has control over her life. She is intelligent, sensitive, active in the political and social life of the community.

The notion of "getting more" is so ingrained in the world-view of people who accept an acquisitive society that the notion of having enough seems almost pathological. To say you are content with a modest but rewarding life can seem like a rejection of your parents. It is often taken by them as a lack of appreciation of how hard they worked to make you better than they are. Yet children don't want to be better than their parents; they want to be themselves. They want to honor their parents for the lives they have led and the struggles they have made, but they don't want their own lives to fall in the shadow of their parents' dreams.

It can be very hard. I know of a carpenter who worked all of his life to send his son to school, and his son decided to become a carpenter and build fine furniture. The father feels he failed to inspire his son; the son feels that by becoming an excellent craftsperson he was honoring his father. They have never been able to communicate this to each other.

Choosing a life's work that is fulfilling and rewarding is a major problem in our society where the things one has and the style one displays are celebrated more than the quality of what one does. Do you work to get stuff, or have you given up the vision of affluence, ease, and "styling" in order to pursue more fulfilling though financially less rewarding ways of being in the world?

Every young person has to confront this choice and, unfortunately, decent advice that validates inner needs and helps them shape a tailor-made future is not easy to find.

. . . .

Get

a Real

Job!

RON DOESN'T have much communication with his father, the director of detectives in a suburban county in northern California. His mother, the administrative secretary of a county supervisor, has never had much sympathy with his aspirations, either. Ron is tall, lean, and full of energy. He was one of the best young actors I'd ever encountered when he was in high school. He loves music, movement, and play. In high school he would juggle in math class, cut civics in order to go to the park and do improvisations with a street theater group. He volunteered to paint sets, go for coffee, sweep floors, and do most anything that local theater people needed—as long as he could hang around backstage for every performance. He also loved to do physical tricks such as tumbling, tightrope walking, standing on his head, and balancing on the back of a chair.

After he graduated from high school Ron had a dilemma. He did well enough to go to a state college but his heart wasn't in it. The theater presented a difficult but intriguing problem. His parents were completely unsupportive. His father refused to talk to him and his mother ranted and raved over dinner about how he was ruining her life and destroying her dreams. Both of them, in less tense moments, urged him to go to college first and play out his theater fantasies later, when he would have a profession in which he could earn a decent living.

Their response reminds me of a story an actor at the Oregon Shakespeare Festival in Ashland told a tour group last summer during the festival. It seems that his father is a surgeon and, even though he is a successful actor in one of the most prestigious repertory theaters in the country, his father would prefer it if he got a "real" job. The theater, it seems, is not a real job like being a stockbroker or doctor or lawyer or CPA. The actor, who clearly has high regard for his father, said that he simply had to get accustomed to the idea that for some people, no matter how successful you are, if you don't work at a standard job, it's not real work.

I go through the same thing myself. Writing, for many people, is not real work. I try to explain that I write for four hours every day, six days a week, have deadlines, have a family, and live a moderately stable life as a writer. Still, it's hard for people who are used to offices and credentials and predictability and sameness to understand that writing, acting, performing music or dance, or painting are disciplines, are real work.

It is very common for people involved in the creative arts and crafts to have relatives and friends advise them to "get a real job" and then do what they care about as hobbies. I heard that growing up, remember adults telling me to become a lawyer or doctor instead of a schoolteacher or a writer, and have heard dozens of versions of it over the thirty years I've been teaching and writing. I still hear it. I remember feeling that the adults around me were rejecting my dreams. It hurt for years, and then it just faded into the realm of silly things people say.

There are many ways of denying the dreams of the young and many little homilies that express that subtle form of rejection. Here are some of them:

- You want to help the poor? Become a lawyer and donate your time. That's better than working in a settlement house.
- You want to be a dancer? You could always dance after you become a CPA. It'll give you the freedom to take lessons. You could even give lessons on weekends.
- You want to build houses? Become an architect. Then you can build a summer house for yourself some day.
- You want to run a restaurant? Get an M.B.A., and when you get rich you can invest in a good French restaurant.
- You want to work in a small print shop? Go to school and learn journalism. You could always buy a small press or computer and produce a neighborhood newsletter in your spare time.
- You want to be a fireman? Good, become an electrical engineer and you can specialize in fire safety. And if you stay in good shape you can become a volunteer fireman.

All of this advice amounts to telling young people to go to college to learn something related to their interests and to take the fantasized "safe" road of getting a degree—when the skills they want to learn are best acquired on the job.

Ron, despite his parents' admonishments, decided to look around and see what he might do that would let him escape college (for him college meant another four years of torture) and do what he wanted, which was to work in the theater. He put up with his parents, tolerated their advice (which he was given not once, but at least a hundred times in his senior year at high school), and as soon as he had his diploma in his hand followed his inner desires and, unfortunately, said good-bye to his parents. He decided that he could not tolerate the idea of not having tried to do what he wanted to do. He decided he'd rather fail than live all his life regretting not having had the courage to try out working in the theater.

Taking risks for your dreams, especially at such a young age, has in my experience always served young people well. It has either determined their life's work or turned them to other ventures without regrets. On the other hand, I know people in their thirties and forties who still dream of breaking loose and trying to live out their vocational dreams. These frustrated aspirations color their current work, which is done somewhat mechanically and is looked upon as worth tolerating since it might buy time in the future. Their present lives are sacrificed for the dream of a future life's work that often doesn't happen.

In 1984, for example, the American Bar Association published a study that claimed that 41 percent of the lawyers in the United States would enter another profession if they could start all over again. I wonder how these people respond to their children's vocational choices.

Ron didn't put off his dreams; he auditioned for the Ringling Brothers and Barnum and Bailey Circus Clown College after he came upon an ad for auditions in the local newspaper. It was not something he ever dreamed of doing, but he felt he had nothing to lose by being auditioned. To his surprise, he got in and became a circus clown for several years. From there he moved to his first love, experimental theater, where he still acts, does rigging, gets coffee brought to him, and is beginning to get his own work produced in workshop settings. His economic needs are modest, and the simpleness of his material life is more than compensated for by the richness of his work and the sense of a camaraderie that he shares with his fellow workers.

Naturally, Ron's life is not for everyone, though he is not unique in his profession. There are thousands of actors in the United States, and, in fact, for the years 1986, 1987, and 1988, according to U.S. Department of Commerce statistics, more money was spent on the arts in the United States than on sports, hard as that is to believe.

Stand Up
for
Your
Children

THERE IS something very important to recognize in Ron's story and the resistance he encountered both at home and in school. Our schools, as currently structured, are designed for one type of person: the conforming test taker. To succeed in school is just about equivalent to being good at taking tests. Yet people like Ron, Karen, and Roger don't care about tests and don't enjoy sitting at a desk. They may become school failures or indifferent students, not because of lack of intelligence or sensitivity but because of the nature of their intelligence and sensitivities. They are resisters who protect that part of themselves that they want to develop in the future; they will not conform and risk losing their own unique strengths in the process. As a consequence, they become problems at home as well as at school because most parents buy the notion that school success is a sign of intelligence and that school failure is a sign of pathology. Too many parents also accept the propaganda that school success is somehow related to success in future life and, often with the best intentions, make themselves and their children neurotic over grades.

Yet people like Ron, Karen, and Roger should be supported, and the school should get the pressure, not the students. It might be difficult to stand up for your child against school authorities, yet doing so, even if it takes time and causes stress, is a gift that she or he will never forget.

Standing up to authority can be very difficult. For example, Cindy, a woman I know, refused to let her daughter, Priscilla, who was a wonderful athlete and a poor and indifferent student, be classified "learning disabled." As a consequence, she had to face the principal, the assistant principal, the guidance counselor, and the county's director of special education, as well as her daughter's teacher. Her daughter was treated rudely by the teacher and was frequently humiliated for not doing well on her work. Cindy persisted and managed to get her daughter transferred to another class. She also got Priscilla a basketball coach and tried in every way possible to help Priscilla develop her athletic skills.

Priscilla learned how to withstand the pressure from teachers and administrators, and she and her mom used to joke that learning to function under pressure would help her in her career in athletics. Priscilla did get a basketball scholarship to college and plans to get a degree in physical education and become a gym teacher. She and her mother are still very close.

Supporting your children when they are in trouble or do something out of the ordinary is a test of your love for them. It's also a test of your own values and flexibility. I've had to learn how to loosen up and listen to my children and understand their inner convictions and aspirations rather than impose my own values on them. Over the past five years my ideas about food, sexuality, and vocation have changed. I've had to look at my own eating habits and have been persuaded that my children's vegetarianism was more sensible than my old Jewish meat-eating habits. I've also come to understand that males and females can share apartments and be friends in ways that wasn't easy or common when I was in my late teens and early twenties, and that young people know a great deal more about safe sex than I did at their age.

I admit that there was a time when I hoped that one or more of my children might go to Harvard, as I did, or at least to Yale. That wish was totally divorced from any sense of what they might want to do when they got there, and my children, as it turned out, had completely different ideas in mind. They made choices that arose from their interests, and have benefited from these choices. I believe that if I had opposed them, our family would have suffered unnecessary and perhaps unbearable stress.

Trust, flexibility, and openness, tempered with honesty, are wonderful high school graduation gifts.

10

Lack of Support and Troubles Within the Family

SOMETIMES THINGS don't work out as well as they did with Priscilla. There are some parents who are more concerned about the opinions of their neighbors and friends than the respect of their children. There are a number of reasons for this, one of which is the way in which parents feel they are personally responsible for problems their children have. A child in trouble supposedly means a deficient parent. Guilt and shame are common parental responses to handicaps in children, and unfortunately they often lead to the intensification of the handicap, turning a manageable problem into a family trauma.

When he was about six or seven, Michael had a mild stutter,

which used to embarrass him. Whenever he felt tense he could hardly talk, but during the usual course of a day it was hard to tell that he had any trouble with speaking. By the time he was in junior high school his stuttering was confined to moments of extreme pressure in school. Whenever a teacher put him on the spot he simply couldn't get the words out in a coherent and comprehensible manner. At home and with his friends he was perfectly at ease with speech. He also loved to read and would sometimes talk himself silently through a book, exercising ways he would read the text out loud. High school was traumatic for him. He was declared learning disabled and hyperactive during his freshman year.

There was one particular teacher who insisted on oral recitals and who in a wry and not completely hostile way liked to mock students who stumbled over a text. Almost all of the students took the teacher's mannerisms as good-natured jesting. However, for Michael it was a constant source of humiliation, and in that class his stutter was as bad as it had ever been. The teacher referred him to the counselor to be screened for learning disabilities, and Michael's response was to refuse to cooperate with anyone he was referred to, including that teacher. In fact, he became defiant and sullen in class and the "learning disability" designation was elevated to include the categories "behavior disorder" and "discipline problem."

Michael became the shame of his family. Because of his stuttering, Michael's parents felt like hiding him every time they had guests to dinner. They considered that handicap as well as his school performance as indications of their imperfection, and thus they resented Michael. His home life was miserable and his school life no better. At school he sulked and was defiant and generally a nuisance. He told me that once they classified him as disabled he decided to act crazy and retarded as a way, he felt, of getting even with them. However, his behavior hurt him more than it did anyone else at the school.

His parents might have been able to help him and find another educational setting where Michael would feel welcome and be able to grow, but they rejected him and resented him.

They kept on telling him that if he didn't cooperate more in school and get some therapy he'd never be able to get into college. They even compelled him to go to several speech therapists, but he refused to cooperate and therefore they couldn't help him. It reached the point where dinner became a funereal event, and Michael said he felt nauseous every time he heard the word *college*. Alternatives to college were never explored and there was no discussion of Michael's interests or dreams. He told one of his friends that he wanted to do something that would help people and thought about working as a volunteer in a hospital. However, that plan never amounted to much, especially after Michael got thrown out of high school in his senior year and ran away from home.

Things had become so bad at home and in school that Michael began thinking of running away. When he got thrown out of high school his parents told him they didn't want him in their house and that he would have to learn how to support himself. He got out all right but didn't go to work. He moved into a homeless encampment.

He knew people there. Michael has a very soft heart and, whenever he could, he would visit people at the encampment and give them cans of soup and clothes meant to go to the Goodwill. It may be that he identified with people at the camp, or that he was genuinely upset that he had so much and they so little, which is what he told me. He also told me that people at the encampment listened to him and didn't care about how he talked. He felt more relaxed and at home there than in the pressure cookers of school and his family. What Michael looked for and needed was support, understanding, and an acceptance of how he perceived the world. He didn't want to be told how he should look at things or how he should talk.

Michael's running away only intensified his parents' shame, and for a while they didn't do anything about it. They lived with the attitude that he'd fail on the streets just as he had failed at school and would come running home. After a month that deception faded, and they still live with the pain of not knowing exactly where he is.

. . . .

Over the years Michael created the fantasy for himself that he wasn't really his parents' child, that they had found him somewhere on some doorstep and regretted taking him in. He had been preparing for years to walk out of the house and not come back or even say good-bye.

What Michael didn't anticipate was the pain and danger of living on the streets. He found himself wandering around panhandling during the days and bedding down in the park at night. He was often sick, hungry, or wasted by crack or cheap wine. He learned to hustle the streets for the little bit of money he needed to keep himself alive and contributed some of it to the community of homeless people who had taken him in and had helped him when he first hit the streets. One couple, in particular, in effect adopted him and saw to it that he did not hurt himself too much. They cajoled him into sharing their food, made sure he kept himself warm, told him who to stay away from, and reminded him that he was not homeless in the way they were. He could go home; they had no home to go to. They taught him how to accept love and generosity as well as give it.

Michael is currently troubled about the choices facing him. Should he go home and deal with the ceremonies of humiliation he knows will occur? Would going home mean admitting failure when he feels that he learned more in a short time on the streets than he had learned all the rest of his life? This is a major conflict for him, since he has decided he wants to work to help the people who helped him, to get the credentials and power to eliminate homelessness. He knows he has to give up the pretense that he can't learn, that he also has to compromise in order to be in a place to be useful to others. He might even have to go to college and take advantage of his parents' offer of support. That would mean going home, and in his heart he doesn't ever want to see "those people." That is the way he refers to his parents whenever family comes up in discussions.

Michael knows he can always stay on the streets, be a freelance social worker, and sell a little dope on the side and use the money he earns to buy food for the homeless. The problem with that, he once told me, is that he would be helping people but he wouldn't be helping solve the whole problem. He knew more than his high school sociology teacher about the challenges of creating decent solutions to social agony.

Whenever I bring up the subject of his parents and the possibility of his going home, Michael tells me to mind my own business. Recently he even told me that our friendship, which has existed for years, would be gone in an instant if I again brought up the subject of his parents. I believe him and intend to keep our relationship going and help him in any way possible.

I don't know what Michael's going to choose; his life is a painful one for himself and for his parents. Michael is beginning to think of getting a job and maybe taking a class or two at the local junior college. However, he likes the streets; they're in his blood now. He knows how to survive, however minimally, in ways few of us could. He is proud of what he sees as his strength and values the friendships he has made. To him the community of homeless people is his family.

Michael has decided that, if he does choose to become a credentialed social worker, he will work with homeless people. He said that if he did go to college it would have to be a place where his experiences and anxieties will be understood and the kind of compassion he feels will drive the learning. Fortunately, there are a number of alternative colleges in the San Francisco Bay Area that credit life experience and encourage a combination of classroom learning and social action. I've been introducing Michael to some of the people who teach at these experimental colleges and hope something will come of it.

For Michael, the choice of a place to learn and a vocation is sensitive, because he has become accustomed to quitting before taking the risk of trying to learn new things. A major problem he and his parents face is where to find useful counsel. If they begin communicating again they might, together, find a way for Michael to define himself in the world and help him feel less homeless while he helps people who have no choice in this society other than to suffer homelessness. I don't know what will happen to him, but though he finds life on the street rewarding, I see him growing too old too fast and worry about his health.

Michael is not a lone instance of someone who feels for others and truly wants to be of use. Unfortunately, people like Michael are often regarded as unrealistic and are told they'll learn better when they get older. They are discouraged in every way possible from devoting their lives to the humane transformation of society. It's fashionable to call people who want to see everyone full and happy "romantics" and mock them for their foolish and utopian dreams. Yet we need more compassionate people like Michael who feel that the fullness of their lives can come from comforting others. Shouldn't we support them and provide ways for them to work with people?

It is essential to support your children, to encourage them to grow in their own ways, and to not feel that you know a safe and sure way to adult success for them. Without that support, families fall apart. Of course, this isn't easy, because it requires seeing your child's life through her or his eyes and not filtering it through your own experience. One way to do this is to imagine what your life might be like if you were the same age as your child and had to make the same decisions she or he has to make.

Imagine

Yourself

a Teenager

Living

in the

1980s

or 1990s

OVER THE past six or seven years my children and students have helped me reimagine the world as if I were a teenager again. Last year in my civics, sociology, and economics class, one of the first things I wanted to do was orient the students to where their homes were in relationship to places they heard about in the news every day. I got a large wall map of the world and the class decided to turn it upside down, or at least I called it upside down. They reminded me that this planet, floating in space, has no up side or down side, or right side or left side. It was, they informed me, all determined by how you looked at our planet from somewhere in outer space.

It was a matter of reorientation, which is what I had to do in order to imagine myself as a high school senior, as one of my own children.

To imagine someone else's world requires temporarily suspending the coordinates and values in your own world. It's hard, or at least it has been hard for me. I know I can't look at my children's future in exactly the way they do, and besides, each of them has a different vision. Still, I just feel that it is essential to try, no matter how tentatively, to understand how they see the world.

Imagine yourself a high school senior in 1989 or 1990. You've done well enough to get into a decent college and through the graces of your parents, grandparents, or scholarship aid you can afford to attend any college you want. Here are a number of questions to try on yourself:

1. What would you want to learn if you had the freedom to choose to learn anything?
2. Whose advice do you take?
3. Do you want to go straight to college or would you like a year or two off?
4. What is there to do in this society that is meaningful to you?
5. How much does meaningful work weigh against dreams of lots of money and future security?
6. What questions do you ask of society?
7. What would you like to learn that you didn't learn in high school?
8. Who would you like to meet?
9. Where might it be fun and interesting working for a year or two?
10. Where would you like to live and how would your room or apartment look?

Become your child or the child you might have been if you were seventeen in 1989 or 1990. Take the time to answer these questions in writing and perhaps even share them with your children and suggest they do the same. Then look at the answers and see what they tell you about what your own children might be thinking.

I asked a friend of mine, Jeremy, who is a corporate lawyer and has a teenage daughter and a twenty-year-old son, to try the questions. Here's what he came up with:

1. I would like to learn something about the ocean, about marine life, about ways of keeping the ocean from being polluted and dead. If I were a kid I'd spend all my time studying the ocean and reading about it.

2. I would look for someone who knew about sea life, maybe go to the university or to the marine biology lab in Bodega Bay, or to the Cousteau Society or Greenpeace. I would just walk in and tell them I'm interested.

3. I wouldn't go straight to college, I'd try to find a place working on the ocean. I'd probably do anything—go on a fishing boat, wash dishes for Greenpeace, clean lab equipment at the marine biology lab. I'd want to get a firsthand sense of what I could do rather than go to college.

4. It's meaningful for me to have enough money for records and some clothes, and to have transportation and to do something that makes me feel good and helps the earth. That's why working on the ocean seems to make sense. It combines what I love with something useful.

5. They both weigh. I don't need lots of money, but I do need enough to be comfortable. I don't want to be a martyr.

6. I want society to let me do the work I care about; I ask it to make me not worry about health care, and not to be prejudiced against me if I decide to do something different as long as I don't hurt anybody.

7. I want to learn how to sail and dive, and collect and study marine life without destroying it. I want to learn about the tides and currents in the ocean and also

about navigation. I want to have some adventures but as a scientist and environmentalist. I also want to learn how to surf.

8. Jacques Cousteau, the Talking Heads, and surfers and divers and sailors.

9. At the Bodega Bay Marine Biology Lab or on a boat— maybe a small salmon trawler if I can't get on a lab ship or the Greenpeace ship.

10. I'd like to keep my room at home and live on a ship or in a dorm with other people interested in the same things as I am. At home I'd have all my records and posters and books, and in the dorm I'd live very simply.

Jeremy told me he got a bit carried away with the exercise and that, in fact, after he turned forty-five he had been thinking about what he would rather have done with his life even before I gave him the questionnaire. He also said that it gave him some understanding of the choice of vocation of his son, Jacob, to which he was thoroughly opposed before. Jacob decided to become a member of the California Department of Forestry's fire service instead of going to the University of California. Jeremy and Jacob fought over Jacob's turning down his place at the University of California, Berkeley, but Jacob won simply by doing what he wanted.

In California there is great need for experienced firefighters because of the number of summer forest fires. Jacob got his first taste of firefighting two summers ago, when he volunteered to join the fire lines during a particularly bad fire. These days he lives on national forest land with a fire crew and is in training to become a professional fire jumper. His dad first resigned himself to Jacob's choice, and now has become proud of his son, whose dream has become his life's work.

The questionnaire Jeremy filled out provides one way of thinking yourself into the world of your own children. Don't think of the way things were when you were young but of the way things are now for your children. Take a nonjudgmental look into your children's world. Try to answer these questions the way you think they would answer them:

- What do they do with their time?
- What do they talk about with their friends or try to share with you?
- What do they like, whom do they admire, where do they enjoy being, and what do they enjoy reading or listening to?
- How do they think about sex and AIDS?
- What are their fears and how do these fears color their hopes?
- How do they think about the role of our country in the world?
- Where do you think they would like to live and how would they like to be living?

Don't fall into the trap of putting down the books and comic books your children respect that you wouldn't read, or the music they like that you wouldn't listen to. Don't mock hair and clothes styles that you didn't grow up with or language you feel isn't expressive enough or gestures that seem foreign and maybe even unmannerly. Try to gentle yourself into the culture of your children. You don't have to like it, imitate it, or embrace it. Find a way to suspend judgment and think your way into your children's world. And remember how many cultural battles exist in the so-called respectable adult community. After all, Mahler's and Boulez's music are as hard for some people to bear as heavy metal or industrial rock, and Daumier and Hogarth upset people with their art during their own times. That doesn't mean you have to like heavy metal—or Mahler, for that matter. It is a question of how you open yourself up in ways that lead to mutual respect within the family, and how you live in a home in which diversity is the norm and mockery of someone else's preferences is considered the equivalent of telling someone that you can't stand someone they are in love with.

Try to take a hard look at who you were as a youngster and

.

5 7

what you might be doing if you were a teenager now. Read books and listen to records that your children find interesting and you might otherwise find foolish or abrasive. And most of all, separate style from substance. What is in the hearts and minds and souls of young people is not fully revealed by the surface. Listen to their words very carefully and make an attempt to define the kinds of problems they are struggling with.

It's important to learn how to resist the temptation to criticize things you don't know or understand, to resist referring your children's experiences back to your own points of reference. Being a parent often requires as much self-discipline of us as we demand of our children.

It's not always easy to be as open as you might like to be. I remember the time my daughter Tonia asked me to stop by a record store to get her a copy of the band the Dead Kennedys' new record, "Nazi Punks Fuck Off." My immediate response was to be appalled by the name of the band. I remembered the sorrows of the assassinations of the Kennedy brothers and how they affected my life. Also the title of the song conjured up images of violence and hatred. It also embarrassed me. How could I go up to a clerk in a respectable record store and say I wanted a copy of "Nazi Punks Fuck Off" by the Dead Kennedys? But I did it, and just as I got the first two words, "Nazi Punks," out of my mouth the clerk told me that the single was one of the best things the band had done for a while and gave me one of the forty or fifty copies sitting next to the cash register.

When I got home I asked Tonia what the record was all about and why the band had such a horrifying name. She explained that I was naive, that the name was meant sarcastically as a comment on American society that killed its best people, and that Nazi punks—violent punks—were giving the punk movement a bad name and so the Dead Kennedys were telling them to fuck off. That seemed quite reasonable to me, only I never could have figured out the meaning the record had for Tonia and her friends by myself.

I graduated high school in 1954, during the McCarthy era. Watching TV was just beginning to be an ordinary experience. The proliferation of nuclear weapons was unthinkable, though we had experienced the exploding of the bombs in Japan and were horrified by it. Radio, the monaural record, and the thirty-five-cent paperback book were central to my self-education. There was the music of Elvis Presley, which somehow led to our parents' talking about how terrible young people were becoming and how they were becoming involved in corrupting and decadent forms of music, dance, hairstyling, and clothes.

For me the jazz world of Charlie Parker, Count Basie, Billie Holiday, and Chet Baker was inspiring, as was the poetry of W. H. Auden and the novels of Sholem Asch and Howard Fast.

All of this seems outdated to my children. In thinking of their perceptions, I have to project myself into a world that is much faster and smaller than the one I grew up in. It is not just videos, microcomputers, electronic music, and instant and condensed world news. I find myself thinking of their cultural choices: twenty-dollar hardback books or two records or three tapes.

My children have flown across the country a half dozen times to visit their grandparents, and feel comfortable thinking about traveling around Europe or Mexico. And I remember my first flight on a propeller plane from New York to Boston. The flight seemed endless and the idea of being so far above the earth terrified me.

I see my children's generation as having a wider, larger view of the world than I have at the same time that they see the world as smaller and every spot on the globe as a place they might visit someday. The wideness comes from the accessibility of different cultures and styles, the smallness from the speed of communication and travel.

There are a lot of complaints these days that youngsters don't know geography, but the world is not so big to them and places are related by styles and events rather than pure landmass. Distances are measured in terms of communication time and not miles. You can see an event on TV as it's occurring in any part of the earth and you might visit even the remotest place if you care to. It's a few hours to London; it's nothing to love black South African music, to listen to Afro-Latin music, English and Irish folk music, Indian ragas, jazz, and, every once in a while, be captured by the magic of Bach. The boundaries between styles and places have been blurred. A world culture is being created and our children are living through its gestation and birth. They have a deeper sense of how events in the world interact with each other than we did. The Vietnam war took place in the United States as well as in Saigon; Russia is alive in everything that happens in Washington, D.C.; the Middle East is in the middle of conflicts people in the United States think and worry about all the time; and the troubles in Northern Ireland are an issue for every Irish-American.

I am often surprised by the way young people worry about the world, whether they are well informed or pick up their information and impressions casually and without analysis. All of them know they are part of a world, not just a country, and are not surprised that events on the opposite side of the world affect them in everyday ways.

12

Dealing

with

Anxieties

About

Your

Children's

Future

IT IS important to examine your own anxieties about your children's future in the context of your sense of where the world will be in the next fifteen years. If you can't figure out what the world will be like then, how can you expect your children to, much less prepare for that world?

What do you think the world will be like in fifteen years? Where would you like to live then given how old you are now and your present conditions? What would you like to be doing and what do you think you will be doing? What are your dreams?

It's important to articulate your dreams because they may

be the same dreams you have for your children and not the dreams your children have for themselves. It is important to separate our dreams for ourselves from the dreams we have for our children, and not to impose upon them the obligation to undo in their lives our own frustrations. They are and must be their own people, and it is on the basis of that independence that love in the family is built.

Think about whether you are trying to guarantee a future for your children when you believe the world has no guarantees. Are you trying to protect them from what they must learn to deal with themselves? I know I am an overprotective parent and my children pay no attention to me in that regard. They do not want me to protect them. They want to feel strong and connected enough to be able to protect themselves and live in a community of mutual regard, protection, and nurturance with their friends. Sometimes the best and most protective intentions of parents can lead to alienation.

It is very important to take inventory of your own values and set priorities regarding what you would like your future relationship to be with your children. Think of them as being twenty-five years old. Most likely, you'll be, as I will, about fifty-five when they reach twenty-five. And think of them as forty, when you will be close to seventy. What do you want your relationship to be then? It is not just for the children to imagine a future for themselves. It is as much a necessary and rewarding exercise of the imagination for us, the parents, to imagine how we will be in the future with them. The long-term relationship between parents and children is much more important than any particular events that happen when children are in their teens. If you keep that long view in front of you, things that your children do that go against your convictions will seem much less troubling. When our children are very young they need our love. When we get older we need theirs, and we have to earn it by our trust and support of them as they grow into adulthood.

Many older friends of mine experience their greatest joy from continuing relations with their children and grandchildren. Others suffer a disease that is practically metaphysical: the refusal of their children to have anything to do with them. Years before, those parents had refused to accept their children's youthful self-definitions; they had felt they knew what was best regardless of what their children felt. There is very little rebuilding possible when the wounds are so deep.

It's also important to remember your own regrets when you think of your children's aspirations. Dreams should be lived instead of simmering under the surface and becoming sources of frustration. Young people are not wrong in slowing down their routes into society and taking time to explore the corners of their desires and the extent of their talents.

What would you have loved to do and where might you be if you never gave up your dreams? Remember, you are asking this question as the seventeen-year-old you might have been, not as you are now. And maybe this is the question your child is facing.

· · · · · · · · · · · · · · · · · · · ·

13

What Would
You Do
if Carl
or Thomas
Were
Your Son?

HIGH SCHOOL graduation is a major time of passage in our culture, analogous to a bar mitzvah, which marks the passage from childhood to manhood. It's interesting that for many youngsters the ideal high school graduation gift is a car—that is, transportation independent of their parents.

All passages are very charged times, and love and separation anxiety, tension, joy, and relief all intermingle in that last moment of high school. It's a time when young people, accustomed to living at home and being fed and sheltered, face independent living. There is usually a mixture of excitement and regret, and the whole tone of graduation is affected by expec-

· ·

tations for the next year. If there is conflict in the family over what the graduate will be doing, or disappointment about not getting into a college or finding the right job, graduation is colored with a sense of failure.

The first day of kindergarten and the last day of high school are the most important school moments for our children. We have to be prepared for both of them so that the passages into and out of school don't undermine our children's faith in themselves and confidence in our love and support.

Here are two portraits of youngsters who have just graduated from high school. Imagine that they are your children. What advice would you give them? Think of their current dilemmas "under the aspect of eternity"—that is, from the point of view of a whole life, not just an adolescent moment. What would you say and how would you act in order to sustain a loving relationship with them all of your lives? Could you imagine ways to undo the bitterness and distance that has developed between these young people and their parents?

CARL

Michael, whose life was described in Chapter 10, ran away from home and ended up in an encampment of homeless people. He has not figured a way out of his dilemmas. He doesn't know how to respond to his parents' rejection and so avoids them altogether. Carl's response to rejection was different than Michael's. He didn't internalize his rejection the way Michael did, and didn't try to hurt himself. Perhaps it was because he had a friend who was going through the same experience and they could share their dreams of leaving home and following their own ways rather than doing what other people wanted them to do. Maybe another contributing factor was that they both loved to work with wood and plastics and to surf and skateboard, and those things brought them into contact with subcultures containing people who had experiences and values similar to their own. Certainly Carl, a skateboarder, was not a loner;

he lived in a culture of peers that had its manners, morals, and language.

Surfers and skateboarders have a loyalty to each other that resembles gang loyalty, though it is much larger and more tolerant. I know youngsters who travel up and down the West Coast surfing and skating. They tell me that it takes at most an hour to hook up with the local community of skaters and surfers and find a place to stay and get a good meal if you can't afford one. In addition, there is a music community that is part of those worlds as well as a number of shops and restaurants that cater specifically to surfers and skaters. If you're hungry and willing to work it is usually possible to find a job at minimum wage and work it into your surfing and skating schedule.

The hedonism of a life of surfing and skating goes against my sensibility. It seems too self-indulgent, indifferent to community affairs, too unstable and limited to the culture of the young. Your body can't last in that world much beyond forty. Nevertheless, the youngsters I know who are part of that world do other things too and have complex dreams of what they will do when they can no longer devote their lives to playing with water and the pavement. In addition, they consider themselves members of a fugitive culture because skateboarding is prohibited in many places and skateboarders are harassed by the police and other local authorities. As fugitives many of them identify with other oppressed minorities, with gay people and with movements against apartheid and U.S. dominance in Nicaragua. It's not unusual to find grown surfers and skateboarders getting into politics or doing community work or becoming teachers or social workers.

For some youngsters, living in a community of peers, feeling oppressed as a member of a group, and feeling solidarity with other oppressed people can become a healthy antidote to terrible family relationships. For Carl, his family was replaced by the world and culture of his friends, and the stronger it was, the less guilt and pain he felt about not having a biological family. The rejected children who survive often do so because they fall into communities of people who have had similar experience and therefore learn to nurture each other at least on a minimal level.

Carl came from a family that is quite well-off and had high ambitions for him. Their dreams had to do with a professional or professorial future and a life of comfort and grace. Carl, in high school, decided that all he wanted to do was surf, skateboard, and listen to music. This didn't sit too well with his parents, who fought with him every night over dinner until he stopped showing up, first for dinner, and then for all meals, until he finally moved out. They accused him of not appreciating all they did for him, and kept on pointing out how their neighbor's son, who got much less from his parents, was one of the best students in high school and got into an Ivy League college. Once Carl left, there was no one to hear their complaints and accusations.

What would you do if your son said he just wanted to take a year or so after high school to surf and skateboard, and also told you that he'd work to support himself so he wouldn't cost you anything? Would you tell him he was ruining his life, or maybe try to bribe or seduce him into going to college or getting a steady job? Or would the fact that he was willing to support himself be enough for you to offer a little help or some suggestions about the kind of creative work he might do?

Carl just managed to graduate from high school. By that time he knew how to repair surfboards and skateboards and, the year after high school, he and his friend opened a small business repairing surfboards and skateboards in his friend's parents' garage. Carl was a master of epoxy and his friend, Charlie, drew cartoons, so they personalized the boards they worked on. After a few years they had a little surf shop on Long Island, and then moved to California together. Carl married and had a son. The shop just about broke even and Carl decided it was time to expand into advertising and sales. He managed to acquire several surfboard franchises and began producing radio advertising for surfboard companies.

What surprised Carl's parents was that he had learned business skills from observing the way his parents did business, when they had thought all along that he was scorning what they did. He just decided to use their knowledge of business in a more modest and less competitive and stressful way.

The success of Carl's advertisements for surfboards, which cleverly mixed surfer jokes and music with a hint of technical expertise, led to his being asked to do a surf music show on the local public radio station. He did the show and added some political commentary. Carl sold the shop to some surfer friends of his and used the money to buy a car. And he pursued a career in radio.

These days he is a producer for a rock and roll radio station in southern California and is doing well enough. He has custody of his son by his first marriage, and his second wife has just given birth to a girl. The two of them seem very happy and content with what, by his parents' standards, would be a minimal life. Unfortunately, he doesn't talk to his parents and they have been deprived of two grandchildren. It seems that neither Carl nor his parents want to swallow their pride and take the first steps toward reconciliation.

Both Carl and his parents hurt, and it's not clear who suffers the greater pain. Nor is it clear why affection doesn't override pride in their case. However, Carl's life is settled and his career in radio is blossoming. I wonder how he'll be with his children. Sometimes it is difficult not to imitate your parents when you become a parent unless you really work at it and have clarified for yourself the kind of parent you don't want to be. I bet on Carl and his wife. They are more full of love than ambition, and their children seem to have a free and yet stable environment with clear limits and lots of support, something neither of them experienced.

THOMAS

There are some school-based problems that create pain in the family. One of them is the so-called problem of dyslexia—that is, difficulty learning to read when there is nothing apparently wrong. Children are identified as dyslexic when nobody can figure out why it is that they don't learn to read with ease. There is nothing intellectual, emotional, or social that can account for dyslexia with the possible exception of bad teaching. However, in our society reading is like a badge of honor. If you can't read you become immediately stigmatized in school. And parents of children who can't read naturally feel guilty, worry about their children's brain physiology, and often go crazy looking for experts and cures to lift the burden of not reading from their children and their family. Yet reading doesn't guarantee a successful life and not reading doesn't have to preclude it.

Michael and Carl had problems with their families and problems in school, which centered around struggles with the authorities. They had no apparent learning problems; they just didn't want to learn from the people who were assigned to teach them. But some students' problems with learning, though maybe caused by bad teaching, become internalized and become struggles with their individual selves.

There are many different ways to approach the problem of dyslexia and many different explanations of what is happening. From my point of view dyslexia covers a multitude of educational sins that become internalized by young people who learn to believe they can't read. It can be caused by anything from missing school for half a year with some illness to being overly logical and not being able to make sense out of phonics for the good reason that, since English is so irregular, phonics in English makes no logical sense.

However it may be caused, dyslexia is often a source of misery in the family. It can lead to self-doubt on the part of the student and parental fear that college entry and future careers will be limited and that such children will be permanently disadvantaged.

What would you do if your child simply failed to learn how to read or didn't care to learn or was so angry with school that whatever was of value to her or his teachers became worthy of scorn and hatred? How would you respond to a child who simply didn't read but in every other way was fine?

·

And how do you think a youngster about to graduate high school would feel if he or she couldn't read despite determined efforts to learn? How would such a young person view the future and deal with the everyday problems of reading directions or newspapers or instruction manuals, much less poetry and fiction? One of the hardest things about dyslexia is that people who are afflicted with the condition often feel they are problems to themselves as well as disappointments to others. For that reason they need every opportunity to develop competencies and skills that take their attention away from an obsession with not reading. In fact, a few years' rest from reading worries often makes it possible for people who had given up on ever learning to read to learn with ease, especially if they have succeeded in some other areas of life.

I've known many families with the problem of dyslexia (it becomes a family problem in most cases). Thomas was told he's dyslexic and he and his family accepted that designation without knowing what it meant, other than that he has had a very hard time learning how to read. He still can hardly read, even though he will be allowed to graduate high school on the basis of taking a purely vocational and remedial program and causing no discipline problems.

Thomas is a graceful athlete, an intelligent and thoughtful person who is delightful to be around. He is also a very accomplished musician and would like to study music, either privately or at a college or conservatory. However, his reading problem seems to block him every time he thinks about applying to some school. He can't fill out application forms or write essays, and is terrified of the SATs.

For Thomas, it all began in first grade, where he had a hard time learning the alphabet and was identified by his teacher as dyslexic. From then on he was in remedial reading classes, going through one remedial program after another, getting progressively frustrated until, by the time he reached high school, he was convinced that he had, as he puts it, "a reading disease." He's afraid to take the written test for a driver's license and so has to depend upon his friends for transportation. He has been channeled into all vocational classes at school even though he would like to be taking more academic classes and would love to be able to read and write. Thomas even went through a period when he was afraid to look up a phone number in the telephone directory.

It's not clear exactly what Thomas's problem is. There is no indication of any thought or brain disorder; he is not psychologically distressed except when it comes to reading, and in conversation he is very clever and insightful. My guess is that he is the victim of bad teaching and early stigmatization in school. He never was in an ordinary reading program and four times was put through the highly structured, thoroughly ineffective behavior modification program, which rewards students with M&Ms. He jokes that he has probably eaten more M&Ms and learned less about how to read than anyone in the history of the school. He reads the sports section of the paper or a music or movie review slowly, carefully, and well when he is with friends, but cannot get beyond the first sentence if he is asked to read the same material in school.

Thomas's dilemma is that he doesn't feel confident enough to think clearly about his future. He also has no idea about how to go about teaching himself to read and acquire the other skills he needs if he is to go to college, play in a band, or try to get a private teacher and prepare for a conservatory. He does read music, however, and that indicates that his reading problem is not impossible to overcome.

So for Thomas the question is how to undo his school experiences. Even with his reading problems he will graduate from high school. It has been set up so that he doesn't have to read in order to graduate. That's not uncommon. If a student is motivated, not a discipline problem, comes from a respectable (in the school administrators' eyes) family, and is a good athlete, most high school administrators will see a way to get her or him a degree, no matter what skills might be lacking.

Thomas has made a difficult decision. He has decided to teach himself how to read and to practice music the year after he graduates. He has a construction job and plans to support himself. His reading plans are to ask friends he trusts to sit and read with him an hour a day. He feels that he can learn more from them than the teachers he has had, and wants a year to distance himself from the regimen of school. His main concern is to be free from the constant feeling of humiliation he had during his school career. Fortunately, he has the support of his parents, who are proud of his musical and athletic ability—and they like him. Their attitude toward adversity is to look for the strength that it can develop. That attitude has served them well; they have had a hard time over the past few years. Their business went bankrupt, and they had to move to a smaller house and work several jobs at a time to keep the family together. Thomas has picked up some of the strength that comes from that kind of optimism.

There are many young people who are the victims of bad teaching and need time away from formal schooling. They also need support and help in articulating plans for their next few years and need to be with people who do not identify school failure with inferiority or disease. Sometimes the solution is very simple, consisting of informal learning situations with supportive people, free of testing, competition, and categorization.

It is much harder when young people give up on themselves, internalize their school failure, and descend into a world characterized too often by drugs, wildness, lack of focus, and fantasies of suicide. This is as true for middle-class youngsters as it is for young people growing up in the ghetto. Self-hatred and despair are not class specific.

For parents the test of love for one's children, as well as one's own personal strength, is most intense when a child feels like giving up on himself or herself. It is precisely at that point when one has to become as intimate and supportive as one has to be with a baby or a two-year-old.

Think what it would be like to be Thomas's parent. What would you have done when school officials told you he had problems in the first grade? How would you push the people at school to become responsible and intelligent in their analysis of his functioning? How would you discover whether they were being arrogant, maybe defensive, or not truthful about what they knew about your child's functioning?

There aren't any simple answers to these questions, but it always seems to come down to whether you quit on your children or whether you are willing to fight for them and stand behind them. This can be difficult if you have troubles of your own to deal with. Nevertheless, strength has to be found, especially in times of passage, when your child is moving from one phase of life to another.

14

Leaving
Home
and
Learning
to Learn

AFTER HIGH school graduation it is easy to feel rejected and pushed out of the nest. It is also natural to feel anxious about the immediate as well as the long-range future. Sometimes youngsters want to stay around home for one more year, or at least a few months, before plunging into college or the world. I remember the anxiety with which each of my children left for college or to work on a project in an unfamiliar community. We all wanted to postpone the actual moment of parting, and adjusting to being apart was difficult. For some youngsters it is just about impossible to leave home right after high school. One of my son's friends who graduated from high school a few years ago wants to be an artist. Ian worked for a local sign painter throughout high school and knew he could get into art school. However, he is an only child and is very close to his parents. They support him in any choice he makes and will always consider him to be at home no matter where he is. As wonderful as this love and support is, it has given Ian a severe case of separation anxiety, which his parents share. They had always done things together and would miss each other very much if he went away to school.

The year after high school Ian simply could not leave home and go off to art school, but he knew that sooner or later he would have to leave. His parents, quite sensibly, didn't push him out, but gentled him out. During the year after he graduated he worked full-time, did a lot of skateboarding, and made a number of trips to the art school he wanted to attend. He also took the time to develop a portfolio and to look at other people's painting and drawing. He had to convince himself that he could make it in a world larger than the small town he grew up in. He had never lived in a community of artists and didn't have any idea of how to measure the quality of his work against that of other talented youngsters. That year he had the time to explore his chosen field without the pressure of classes and grades. He built up confidence, sorted out art schools, tested different media, and worked. The time was not wasted. On the contrary, it was a time of consolidation, a time to gather the strength and courage he needed to test his art and take on the challenge of living in a city for the first time.

A year later, Ian enrolled in art school and moved to San Francisco. He made visits home as often as possible. At school he made new friends and found art school very rewarding, though he's already thinking of taking his third year off and traveling around Europe skateboarding and looking at paintings. However, he definitely plans to spend the second year continuing his art studies.

I've known other youngsters like Ian who needed a year to breathe, and a year to say good-bye to home. There's nothing unhealthy about that when there is a goal in mind and a youngster isn't just hanging around watching TV or drinking beer or smoking marijuana. If your child has a genuine need for a prolonged good-bye and at the same time is trying out new skills and preparing to do something specific in the future, that year might be a wonderful gift. One has to consider very carefully the degree to which unwillingness to leave home is a form of giving up or a way of gathering strength and practicing skills for the future. It's probably best to talk explicitly about the child's reasons for wanting to hang around, and to spend time exploring vocational choices with your child if he or she seems to be lost or scared. In most cases, halfway through a year at home, boredom will set in; that is the time for the youngster to invest in visiting places where he or she might like to work or attend school.

If, on the other hand, boredom and fear of leaving home seem to be turning into self-destructive behavior and paralytic functioning, it is probably advisable to seek some counseling.

Some students have the opposite desire. They have wanderlust and find ways to leave high school early (through taking either additional classes or a high school equivalency test), work a bit, and then travel. For some the travel can become a way of life for years and may eventually lead to a choice of vocation that involves being on the road. Alice is like that. She lives with her mother and did well in high school but couldn't stand it. She decided to take her high school equivalency exam and spend what would have been her senior year working as a maid and waitress until she had enough money to travel in Europe for a few months. When she got back from Europe she had to face the great open space of her future. What could she do? What did she want to do? For her, college was not a place to find answers, and so she went back to work and played around with her dreams. The dreams ranged from being a world traveler and translator for the United Nations to writing romance novels, running a small crafts shop, driving a bus, or becoming an international lawyer working on issues of justice for children. It was wonderful to watch her imagination run wild. She went from the scale of the world to a modest shop in a tourist town of five thousand people.

Alice's mother, Rebecca, is a single parent who has no independent income and works very hard to support her three children. The expenses of everyday life consume her resources even though she earns what would be considered a decent middle-class salary. It's not easy raising three children by yourself in any city.

Alice has been out of high school for two years now, and at nineteen is beginning to focus in on several vocations. She has learned how to make enough money to support herself through working in shops, supermarkets, hotels, restaurants, and motels—though she hates the work. As she told me, the only interesting thing about the jobs is people-watching or speculating about the people she cleans up after from the things they leave behind. And, she added, after a while that becomes boring as hell, too.

Alice has had time to reflect on what she might do with her life—perhaps too much time, because she has a tendency to delay making any commitment in case another opportunity or possibility arises unexpectedly. She has been to Europe several times and has learned French and Spanish. She has also made friends in Europe and been influenced by their left-wing politics in ways that cause her frustration in the United States, where she sees no genuinely progressive national movements. She wants to be part of making a decent world and can't figure out how to work on that, support herself, and do interesting work all at the same time. Fortunately, her mother finds Alice's aspirations wonderful and they have a very close, loving, and respectful relationship.

Alice's current plans are to learn as many languages as she possibly can and find a way to travel by being a translator. She's contacted the Berlitz language schools and found that there is a possibility that she can teach English for them throughout the world as she learns other languages. She has no problem working and learning at the same time, no resistance to going to college if it makes sense, and no desire to go unless it fits into her plans for herself. She also has decided not to worry about what she will be like when she is fifty years old, though occasionally she does have some anxiety about the future. She wants to develop the skills to mold her future so that when she is fifty she feels as free and positive as she does now.

Alice's mother supports her in all of her efforts and they thoroughly enjoy each other's company. Of course, Rebecca is a bit anxious about Alice's future, but that doesn't interfere with her relationship to her daughter. In fact, they both joke about the uncertainty of both of their futures, and feel proud of their mobility and ability to support themselves while feeling free to travel and learn.

Alice has just returned from her latest trip to Europe and is about to enroll in an international college program that will give her the opportunity to take advantage of campuses in many different parts of the world. She intends to study inter-national relations and languages and hopes eventually to do some work that involves traveling and gives her the freedom to write novels. The years she has spent traveling and working have given her a maturity that very few college juniors have. She is well-read and aware of things of this world that are hard to come by in college. She loves to share her experiences and is delightful to be with. For Alice, life on the road was a very good choice. When she was a junior in high school she was unhappy, angry, and often self-pitying. She's grown out of that part of herself and sees the future as an exciting adventure. Her way of living after high school is not for everyone, but some youngsters, with support from home, can find their life's work on a world scale.

It's been a privilege for me to be able to follow young peo-ple as they find their places in the world in nonordinary ways. It has been particularly interesting when they have the kind of support that Alice has, since family conflict, guilt, and anxiety do not cloud the voyage. Sometimes it's very difficult to support your children when they do things that have no relationship to your own experiences. I know that I try to draw upon my life in order to understand the lives of my children, and often come up empty. Their anxieties are not the same as mine. My wife and I have had to become students as well as advisers, and our children have always been willing to teach us about their world when we've shown interest. That doesn't mean that we pretend to be part of their world or to like things we don't like; decent and respectful disagreement is part of the development of sustaining love, and now I welcome it, whereas there was a time when I believed too much in my own way of seeing the world and closed my eyes to the complex views of other, often younger, people.

The problems young people will face, even with family support, are the problems we all face trying to make our way in a thoroughly imperfect world. Two of my former students, Jay H. and Jay L., have traveled together for years. With the support of their families they have been working, studying, trying to find ways to make a decent world and steal some fun along the way for over fifteen years and are none the worse for their adventures.

Jay H. knocked on the door of our house in Berkeley about seventeen years ago. He wanted us to sign a petition dealing with some environmental issue. I invited him in and asked him to explain the issues, which he did with eloquence. I was in a combative mood and decided to challenge his position even though I agreed with it. Jay H., who is very tall and gentle, dealt with me patiently and pursued all of my objections with a logic I could not resist. I finally gave in, told him I agreed with his position, and, to change the subject, asked him what he was doing in school. He told me he had just decided not to go to college because high school was boring and his teachers refused to answer his questions.

At that time I was the director of a public alternative high school and taught classes in writing, psychology, philosophy, and politics. I suggested that Jay H. drop around the school and see if he might like to be a part of some of the classes. He became one of our students and later told me that he found an environment there where his questions were taken seriously and his mind and opinions were respected.

Jay L. came to the school in another way. He had dropped out of high school in order to learn how to repair motorbikes and read the books he wanted to read rather than ones he was assigned to read. He was a quiet rebel, someone who withdrew from participation rather than confront his teachers.

Jay L.'s mother, who felt he was right in dropping out, had heard of our school and she brought him around. He immediately hooked up with Jay H. They were kindred souls with free-ranging minds, a healthy disrespect for authority, and a desire to know as much as possible about how the world worked. They also refused to be graded, tested, classified, or categorized. On the other hand, there was no interesting intellectual, mechanical, or artistic challenge they retreated from.

The Jays were at the school for two years, and during that time they participated in philosophy, literature, and mathematics classes; were involved in a sailboat-building project; and worked at a ceramics studio throwing pots. They also persuaded me to teach a cooking class at my home once a week during the evening, and they became more competent at cooking than I am. By the end of the class I had to bring in guest chefs and become one of the students.

When they graduated they decided to take off across the country for a year and then see something of the world beyond the United States. They reached the East Coast and decided to continue across the Atlantic. They earned their way to Europe by washing dishes, repairing motorcycles, doing construction work, selling their ceramics. After a while in Europe they returned to California and worked some more while becoming involved in antinuclear and antiapartheid activities. Then they split up for a while. Jay H. spent a year at the London School of Economics studying political and economic theory, and Jay L. spent a year at a California university studying computer science. When they learned as much as made sense to them at that time, they dropped out and became involved in setting up small businesses for poor people. They had the skills to help set up bicycle, motorcycle, and auto repair shops; to develop small contracting firms; and to do ceramics. They also knew computers, could do bookkeeping and accounting, and had a commitment to being useful to other people. For them college was a temporary episode, a place to acquire skills that could be used to help create a more decent society.

In our society what the Jays are doing seems unusual, yet in Europe many young people travel, are involved in political activity, move in and out of the universities, and do many different kinds of work. When it comes to young people between the ages of seventeen and twenty-four, we are much more anxious to push them into the job market than people are in Western Europe, where there is much less of a rush to "grow up" and "settle down." Though the majority of young people in Western Europe do not live like the Jays, a substantial minority do, and their form of life is not considered unusual.

I think it would be greatly to the benefit of our culture and the quality of our lives to let up a bit, slow down, learn more, and acquire less. There's nothing wrong, for example, in taking a year off from college to travel or do community or environmental work or manual labor. The more experience young people have, the more sensibly they can use educational opportunities and integrate what they learn with what they do.

The years between seventeen and twenty-four are good times to explore the world, to try one's hand at different jobs and crafts and arts, to acquire a variety of skills and build up a repertoire of possible careers. Why rush into a job, or try to graduate as early as possible and go right on to graduate school or into a corporation, when those years would better be used to build skills and the internal foundation for intelligent citizenship and a sustaining, decent, and rewarding life?

. . . .

A Note on Taking Time Off During College and Figuring Out What to Do After College

BEING IN college does not make one immune from the doubts about one's life work and future that high school graduates often have. In fact, finding oneself about to be a junior in college without any sense of what to do after senior year can become a continual source of anxiety. It seems that more and more college students are taking the option of a year off from college to explore just the things I've been suggesting high school graduates might be doing instead of going directly to college. In fact, many colleges encourage students to break their college careers and take a year to travel or explore vocational possibilities. I've talked to counselors at a number of colleges, ranging from Harvard, Reed, and Wesleyan to the University of Michigan and the University of Texas, Austin. They felt that for some students a year off was an appropriate choice, one that might help them focus on how to make use of their remaining years in college. One thing they also agreed upon was that it was not sensible to take off that year between one's junior and senior years. They said the best time to take a year off was between the sophomore and junior years. The second-best choice was between the freshman and sophomore years. They felt that the last two years should be done consecutively, leading as they do to a thesis and to a finer definition of what to do after college.

I've known a number of youngsters who've taken time off to do things in the world during their college careers. One, Joan, went to a state university after graduating from high school. The university was very difficult to get into and very large. Her classes usually had several hundred students and she felt very alienated the first few months. She couldn't find anyone on the faculty to talk to about her academic interests and found that the graduate students who ran the small sections of her large classes were worried about their own Ph.D.s and didn't want to be bothered with the concerns of undergraduates. In addition, she was homesick.

Joan did well in her first year but felt she wasn't going anywhere. College was worse than high school because it was colder and the professors were more distant than her high school teachers. She couldn't explore the fields she was interested in because she had to take general education classes. She didn't mind taking them, but was frustrated because she wasn't able to take classes in the field she thought she might like to work in, anthropology.

Joan wanted to learn what kind of work anthropologists do other than teaching anthropology. Her goal, not at all clearly articulated, was to study, in respectful ways, cultures very different than the one she grew up in and to use that knowledge and her goodwill to help people less fortunate than she was.

As a freshman she set up an interview with the anthropology department chairperson, who told her she would have to wait until the end of her sophomore year to get counseling on the nature of work in the field of anthropology. Her freshman adviser told her she had time to worry about what she was going to do with her life after she graduated from college. She was advised to concentrate on her work at college and think about her major, not her future.

Joan didn't feel that she had that grace period and also didn't want it. She wanted to learn about the study of culture and develop skills that might be useful in underdeveloped parts of the world as soon as she could. She wanted to major in anthropology as a tool, not as an academic study. Her desire to work in the undeveloped world was greater than her desire to wait for what the academic study of anthropology would offer her. For a while she did wait, until she realized that she was not being given access to what she wanted to learn because of the structure of the university's programs.

Many students find themselves blocked that way. At the moment they are ready to commit themselves to a certain field and discover whether they want to give their lives to a certain area of knowledge or action, they are told to wait until they do what is required of them. Of course, there are good arguments for a liberal education, for a broad-based education, but why concentrate it at the beginning of college? It seems more sensible to me to integrate larger views once one has had a chance to play in smaller fields. I would like to see required humanities, science, and cultural classes spread throughout a college career rather than "gotten over with" during the first two years. After all, the more one brings to classical and technical studies, the more one is likely to take away from them.

Joan was impatient with what she was required to take. She had a personal agenda to explore and it nagged her throughout her second year at college. After her sophomore year Joan couldn't figure why she was still in college other than that, according to her parents and high school teachers, it was a prestigious place to be and graduating would guarantee her a good job in the future.

She decided to take a year off to explore some activities in "the real world" and spent the summer living at home and working to accumulate money so she could buy a year to explore things she cared about. She wrote dozens of letters to organizations she had read about in magazines and academic journals and ended up with several offers to join digs in Latin America if she could pay her way.

The kind of persistence Joan showed usually pays off. It's possible to find a way into almost any profession or occupation as a volunteer or apprentice if you keep following leads and go straight to the source and ask to become involved. I've known young people who've managed to get themselves into science labs, theater troupes, music groups, law offices, and many other places simply by hanging around, trying to be of use and following advice and leads.

Joan chose to volunteer for an anthropological study she found advertised in a magazine. Before she went she researched the area and language of the people she would be studying. She spent a year in Latin America working with indigenous people while studying their culture, and managed to travel a bit as well. After that year she transferred to another college, where there was a good anthropology department, and is thinking about becoming an anthropologist with a specialty in Latin America. She also decided to take a minor in community development so that she could temper her study of people's cultures with service to them. She heard about her new college from another young person who was on the trip with her.

Joan learned what many other young people learn, which is that the best source of information is often your peers and the most indifferent source of help about your future is, too often, the people paid to give you advice.

When Joan graduated from college she spent several years working in Latin America with a research group from an eastern university that had a grant from the Ford Foundation. Her specialty was studying the role of agriculture in rural Ecuador and the development of new food crops (in particular, soybeans) using traditional agricultural methods. She's now enrolled in a doctoral program and plans to return to Latin America in a few years.

Not everyone has Joan's sense of purpose and direction. For some people even graduating from college and getting into graduate school can leave the question of vocation hanging. I know that when I was studying philosophy in graduate school at Columbia University I felt it was all wrong. I enjoyed philosophy but didn't want to be a professor. I wanted to be an elementary school teacher working in a public school. Why, I don't know, but that's what my heart told me. It took three years after graduating from college and two graduate schools for me to go with my feelings and get an elementary school teaching credential.

Rose, the daughter of a friend of mine, has a similar dilemma. Rose attended first-rate schools all of her life and did very well. But her dream was to be a jazz singer: She sings or hums all the time and she dreams music. When she graduated from high school she took a year off to try to make it as a singer. She was supported by her family and took voice and piano lessons. Some friends of the family had contacts in the music business and she became a backup singer in a group that was just beginning to develop a local reputation.

During her year with the group she met many other singers and began to realize that she didn't have that special unique sound and obsessive commitment to music that might lead to success. Her love of music never diminished, but her desire to have a career as a musician disappeared. She entered college and used the money she had earned singing to supplement her scholarship and what her family was able to provide her.

Last year she graduated from college and decided to go to law school. She loves legal briefs the way she loves music scores—a strange, perhaps unique, combination of complexities. But she didn't want to give up music. With her unusual combination of creative and analytic thinking she has figured out a way to integrate music and the law. She has decided to be a lawyer in the music industry, and many of the young musicians she knew when she was performing have told her that she can be their agent, lawyer, or manager once she gets her law degree. And she knows she can sit in with them anytime she feels a need to sing.

Sometimes one simply cannot do things one loves well enough to devote a life to them. There are people who want to write who can't find a written voice, people who want to be athletes who don't have the body or coordination to sustain a career in professional sports. There are other people who would rather be artists but have inelegant lines, be filmmakers but don't have visual sensitivity. There are gifts that sometimes allow dreams to become vocations, and there are dreams without gifts that can be constant sources of frustration. Nevertheless, it is possible to take your vocational love and integrate it with what you *can* do well. I know people, too short to play basketball, who have become part of basketball teams as business managers and accountants, people who wanted to be artists who work in galleries, people who would rather be scientists but become managers of scientific corporations. These options may not be the fullest realizations of their dreams, but proximity with what they love has provided a great deal of pleasure in their lives. There are indirect ways to realize your vocational dreams as long as you can articulate them. Life's work can sometimes realize and often approximate life's dreams.

16

Education

and

Values

THE TWO Jays, Joan, Roger, and the other young people I've described in earlier chapters are struggling with moral questions, questions of what is right and wrong and of what there is to do that is of value in the world. They are trying to discover, on an emotional and intellectual level, where they stand on political, social, and vocational issues. They do not separate vocation from value, and at this stage in their lives resist the idea that you do work in order to buy time to do good works or please yourself. They want to integrate emotion, morals, work, and community. They want to be within the world rather than work, live, play, and keep all the parts of their lives in compartments. It is definitely a romantic dream, but not the less admirable for that.

Their quest and exploration of values is appropriate throughout life, but particularly appropriate when one is about to graduate from high school and leave home. At that moment young people in our society feel an enormous, possibly exaggerated, weight to the decisions they have to make about their futures. High school graduation is truly a commencement, a beginning of a new way of being in the world. It is a time of passage, and at such times the moral questions are the most important ones. Who one shall be, what one shall value, and how one can sustain love and do rewarding work are the central obsessions of the last days of high school.

The young people I have described are struggling with questions of identity in more conscious ways than many other people of their age. They worry consciously about issues as diverse as social justice and personal identity and find themselves withdrawing from the conformity and competition that characterizes high school life in the United States.

They also think about the contradictions between conforming and competing and the sham that is created by a social world in which you are both honored for being like everyone else and told that you have to be number one. These youngsters are sometimes on the edge and sometimes in the middle of the social and cultural worlds of their high schools and yet aren't fully part of them. They look at themselves and the world they live in and reflect. They are sociologists and philosophers and don't know it.

I remember when I was in high school my school sent me to Empire Boys State, which was sponsored by the New York State American Legion. There were high school students from all over the state at the meeting, and we were supposed to have mock presidential conventions and develop candidates and platforms. We were divided into two parties, and caucuses were set up. On the convention floor we were provided with balloons and confetti. We were to imitate the adult two-party system, but no serious social issues were to be addressed.

There were a number of us who resisted the whole process, who couldn't cheer and felt foolish throwing confetti. We couldn't support the platform of any person who had no positions but was just pretty and slick in some conventional way. And instead of becoming a caucus we became friends and spent evenings talking about our values and futures, not about winning a silly game that led to a certificate from the American Legion.

The adults running the mock convention became very angry with us because we wouldn't play their games, but we didn't play them at high school either. We were no different from Karen or Michael or the two Jays. We were trying to define ourselves in a hostile world and at the same time find ways to be decent to others. We couldn't play the game.

The young people I've described in these vignettes don't even accept the legitimacy of the game, though in small ways they may make concessions and play a bit to it. The themes that come up when these young people talk about their aspirations are service, meaningful work, and a desire to remake a society they do not respect. Cooking, construction, film and other media, music, small independent business, the microcomputer world, the arts, teaching, the caring professions, public service, environmental and community work, and theater and the arts are often central to their dreams. Helping people who are poorer than they are, guilt for the privilege they have been born into, and longing for relevance as well as cynicism toward the politics and materialism of the larger society characterize the values they express.

All of the media talk about youngsters caring only for money and all of the put-downs of high school and college students who are supposedly greedy and self-centered are contrary to my experience with young people. I have found them as compassionate and thoughtful as young people were during the civil rights movement and during the 1970s. It is just that they have no movement to relate to, no single style they want to adopt. And they have to deal with an adult political and social climate that is, in fact, stupid (witness the last presidential election campaign), greedy, and self-serving—one that, on a national level, is indifferent to the sufferings of small people. They have no leaders or heroes, though there are musicians and actors they admire for their courage in speaking out through the arts. The worldwide appeal of the Live Aid and Amnesty International concerts, and the dozens of walks and runs and skateboard contests for peace, as well as the local and national environmental activist groups in which young people play a part, indicate that we don't have an indifferent and greedy generation of young people. Instead, there are many young people struggling to find ways to solve some of the more difficult problems of the planet and letting their voices be heard in opposition to the dominant voices in adult society, no matter how tentatively.

The sensitivity and seriousness of these young people who won't play the money game and won't allow themselves to be told that they are personally responsible for the world's social, sexual, economic, and racial problems might help all of us heal some of the wounds that characterize our life on the planet. After all, in the world today the children are moral leaders. Think of South Africa and Palestine, and remember that the sit-ins and demonstrations that led to the desegregation of the South in the United States were driven by young people who, by taking the risks they did, led the adults.

The youngsters I am talking about are not themselves part of any social movement, though a number of them are longing for a movement that will take another step toward social and economic justice. Most of them are middle-class; many of them have different values than their families. Others wish they could be as involved as their parents were in the 1960s and early 1970s. They long for a present that they create and do not want to live in their parents' dreams or reminiscences.

What these young people have in common is a desire to be of use to themselves and to a larger world as well. College is an epiphenomenon to them, an incidental stop that might be useful as a step on the way toward a full and meaningful life but that has no intrinsic value. They don't buy into the college game and have made the decision to create their own lives out of the possibilities that are available. I feel we adults can only admire them and feel hope, for the world of the future will emerge from their discontent.

Yet what is available other than college for a sixteen- or seventeen- or eighteen-year-old who can go to college and whose parents want him to go to college and who has a consuming desire to do something other than more school right after high school?

It's worth exploring.

part two

. . . .

How to Set Up and Use a Career Profile

Elective
Affinities

I REMEMBER when I was still in elementary school I would sit inside my house in the Bronx and look out of the window at the dirty snow on the street. Children weren't allowed to go outside in that weather because the common knowledge of the time was that you could get polio from the dirty snow. I used to complain all the time that there was nothing to do inside and pity myself for my boredom. My relatives must have had their fill of my moanings and groanings, for one day my grandmother said, "OK, you can paint or draw, read a book, play the accordion, or wash the dishes and clean the toilet." She taught me about options. There was no option to do nothing, because by doing nothing I was a problem to everyone else, which was doing something.

The reason I begin this section with that story is that I have heard many high school students say, in that same bored voice I once used, "What can I do with my life?" For example, recently I asked one of my high school writing students what kind of things she might like to do with her life, and after thinking for a bit, she said, "I can't say what I want to do because I don't know what there is to do."

What *is* there to do, and where does a young person find out about possibilities? If college is the choice it's not too difficult to obtain many sources of information, ranging from private counseling to college catalogs and dozens of guidebooks to colleges. However, even with respect to choosing a college, high school seniors face some major frustrations. They can easily find out what colleges are rated "good," how much it costs to attend, and what kind of grades and scores they need to get in, but what about the choices there are when one gets there? How do high school seniors learn what it means to be a sociologist, a political scientist, a microbiologist or ethologist? How could they discover the difference between cybernetics and pharmacology, or cultural anthropology and audiology? How would they know what it is possible to do?

Most U.S. high schools live in the past. They do not teach current literature, music, science, technology, or mathematics. They have sparse or nonexistent art and cultural programs. They do not provide opportunities for students to sample the things they might do with their lives.

Unfortunately, many people who make educational policy and determine the content of high school curriculums have a narrow vision of what it is important to learn, and limit the content of what is presented in high school to bland and obsolete ideas and classroom-based experiences that have nothing to do with the larger experience provided by travel, work, and learning in the world outside of school.

Too few educators believe that the role of high school should be to encourage diversity and the exploration of life's possibilities. There is little encouragement for the development of active minds and imaginations. As one high school student I know said to me recently, if Socrates taught at his school the administration probably wouldn't offer him poison but he'd be fired for sure.

Finding out what one might be able to do in the future is a central concern of high school students, many of whom are afraid that they will never have time to discover what they would love to do with their lives. Many young people in our society worry that they might have to resign themselves to meaningless, competitive, somewhat boring work in order to earn money and try to do what they enjoy outside of work. Work becomes a job instead of a vocation, and most adults tell young people that dull work is the nature of life.

I disagree!

We need to provide a creative vision to young people of how life can be lived fully and wonderfully. Certainly everyone will experience some pain and frustration along the way, no matter what, but there is no need to set out safe, boring paths for young people. We need to help them explore what can be done in the world rather than tell them what we believe can't be done.

The opportunity to discover what you might love to do and make central in your life is more important during the last years of high school than worrying about what college you get into.

One way to approach the question of vocation is to explore the elective affinities young people might feel for a particular form of work. *Elective Affinities* is the name of a book by the German author and thinker Goethe, and it refers to the concept that people live most fully when they understand the aspects of life and work that they have natural affinities for, and build their lives around these affinities. An affinity is a feeling, almost a passion, for a way of living and acting. For Goethe, "a teacher who can arouse a feeling for one single good action, for one single good poem, accomplishes more than he who fills our memory with rows upon rows of natural objects, classified with name and form."

The search for vocation, for direction in one's life, is based upon a feeling of affinity, of belonging, of doing work and living in a way that brings out one's inner resources. Definition of career and vocation comes from within, not from a list of recommended jobs. The exploration of affinities is much more important than any specific training one can get, and time spent learning how you want to live is time gained, not time wasted.

Some people feel a need to work with other people; others prefer to work with animals or in the natural environment. Some people love building things or experimenting with machines or materials. Still others enjoy creating works out of the magical elements of color, sound, movement, fiber, and stone. There also are some people who love to manage or sell, to nurture the creative processes of others, and to organize things for effective functioning. There are many ways people can take pleasure in their work, whereas the frustration and pain of spending most of your adult life doing something you would rather not do can be enormous.

Here are some ways to explore affinities with teenagers. The goal is to help young people find out where their hearts lie and use that knowledge to determine the vocation they might like to pursue. I've focused on five particular areas of work and explored ways young people can become actively involved in testing out the vocational aspirations they imply. There are, of course, other areas of work, and it's impossible to cover them all in one book. Consequently, later in the book, I've provided suggestions on how to create your own profiles for any area of work.

The areas of work I've chosen to examine are:

1. Work with People
2. Work in Media and the Arts
3. Ecological and Environmental Work
4. Work with Animals
5. Work with Things (building, inventing, and experimenting)

For each of these forms of work, I have created a profile form that

- tries to cover the variety of careers opened up by it
- lists the kinds of places, such as hospitals, parks, or laboratories, where the work is done
- describes the roles different people play in a particular job situation
- suggests specific ways in which young people can get involved with testing out these careers during the last years of high school and the year after high school graduation

The suggestions provided here are based on the assumption that the exploration of career affinities, of the definition of areas for a life's work, can be a family affair and doesn't need the input of a professional counselor. There are a number of differences between going to a professional counselor or high school counselor and doing one's own counseling in a family setting. One doesn't usually have to set up an appointment to speak to somebody at home, or pay for time by the half hour, or be rushed out of the office because other people are waiting. Questions that arise can be answered over breakfast or discussed on the weekend. Follow-up calls and visits can be planned at one's convenience. There also is considerably more flexibility at home, and more opportunity to draw other people, such as friends and business associates, into the counseling process.

However, if one isn't alert this flexibility can be a source of trouble. When counseling can take place at almost any time it can easily be postponed or put off. The more people involved in the process, the more difficult it is to keep track of where one is in the process.

In addition, the emotional dynamics of family life are bound to play a role in counseling sessions that do not depend upon an outside professional. If the relationship between parents and children is very tense, if they cannot speak to each other without ending with a shouting match or tears, it's going to be difficult to focus on the single purpose of getting together to help a teenager decide what she or he would like to explore as potential lifelong work. On the other hand, if parents accept a supportive and advisory role in the counseling process, and leave the decision making to the youngsters themselves, emotional support within the family can make the passage from high school into the larger world a positive and fruitful experience leading to an interesting future.

The following five profile forms will be analyzed in the book. You might want to peruse them before going on. Then try to imagine how you might make use of them to explore the choice of meaningful work. If you come up with any strategies or suggestions that you do not find in the next parts of the book, incorporate them in your explorations, and please let me know about them so that they can be added to future editions.

WORK WITH PEOPLE

Ages of People to Work With	Life Conditions of the People to Work With	Areas of Work	Ways You Can Become Involved
A. Infants	A. "Normal"	A. Social welfare	A. Volunteer work
B. Early childhood (2 to 5)	B. Economically needy	B. Education	B. Summer work
C. Young children (6 to 12)	C. At risk	C. Politics	C. Apprenticeships
D. Teenagers	D. Mentally ill	D. Legal issues	D. Entry-level work
E. Grown-ups	E. Physically ill	E. Recreation	E. Semiskilled and skilled work
F. Seniors	F. Handicapped	F. Study of people	F. Independent study
	G. Gifted	G. Travel	
		H. Caring for others	
		I. Medicine	
		J. Nutrition and food preparation	
		K. Transportation	
		L. Public safety	
		M. Environment	
		N. Ergonomics	
		O. Communications and media	
		P. Organizing	
		Q. Arts	
		R. Sciences	

PROFILE FORM #1

WORK IN MEDIA AND THE ARTS

Areas of Work	Modes	Places of Work	Ways You Can Become Involved
A. Writing	A. Creation	A. Studio	A. Volunteer work
B. TV and radio	B. Performance	B. Business	B. Summer work
C. Film and video	C. Direction	C. College/school	C. Apprenticeships
D. Photography	D. Design	D. Community center	D. Entry-level work
E. Music	E. Technical crafts	E. Home	E. Semiskilled and skilled work
F. Theater	F. Editorial	F. Organizations	F. Independent study
G. Dance	G. Criticism	G. TV/radio network or station	
H. Fiber arts and fashion	H. Production	H. Theater	
I. Painting and printmaking	I. Administration	I. Production center	
J. Sculpture and 3-dimensional art	J. Publicity and sales	J. Craft fairs	
K. Industrial and commercial design	K. Running a venue		
L. Jewelry, glass, and ceramics	L. Manager/agent		
M. Crafts	M. Manufacturing		

PROFILE FORM #2

ECOLOGICAL AND ENVIRONMENTAL WORK

Focus of Work	Types of Work	Places of Work	Ways You Can Become Involved
A. Water	A. Research	A. Urban	A. Volunteer work
B. Land	B. Documentation	B. Rural	
C. Minerals	C. Communication	C. Wilderness	B. Summer work
D. Atmosphere	D. Advocacy	D. Laboratory	
E. Man-made goods	E. Care/maintenance	E. Advocacy group	C. Apprenticeships
F. Waste management	F. Recreation	F. Fund-raising organization	D. Entry-level work
G. Plants/trees	G. Emergency services	G. Government agency	
H. Wildlife	H. Medical/health	H. Corporation	E. Semiskilled and skilled work
I. Human ecology	I. Conservation	I. Community group	
J. Energy	J. Preservation	J. School/college	F. Independent study
	K. Restoration	K. Museum	
	L. Recycling and disposal	L. The "field"	
	M. Agriculture		
	N. Aquaculture		
	O. Horticulture		

PROFILE FORM #3

WORK WITH ANIMALS

Focus of Work	Types of Work	Places of Work	Ways You Can Become Involved

A. Land animals
  1. free
  2. domesticated
  3. trained
  4. captive
B. Water animals
  1. free
  2. domestic
  3. trained
  4. captive
C. Birds
  1. free
  2. domestic
  3. trained
  4. captive
D. Insects
E. Reptiles
	A. Study of animals
	B. Preservation
	C. Conservation
	D. Restoration
	E. Advocacy
	F. Legal issues
	G. Training
	H. Breeding
	I. Farming
	J. Care
	K. Health/nutrition
	L. Competition
	M. Commerce
	N. Emergency rescue/disaster management
	O. Education
	P. Control
	Q. Art/photography/film/video
		A. Wilderness
		B. Urban
		C. Rural
		D. Laboratory
		E. Zoos
		F. Veterinary clinics, medical facilities
		G. Kennels/boarding
		H. Training schools
		I. Pet shops
		J. Circuses
		K. Organizations and advocacy groups
		L. Government
			A. Volunteer work
			B. Summer work
			C. Apprenticeships
			D. Entry-level work
			E. Semiskilled and skilled work
			F. Independent study

PROFILE FORM #4

WORK WITH THINGS
(BUILDING, INVENTING, AND EXPERIMENTING)

Focus of Work	Types of Work	Places of Work	Ways You Can Become Involved
A. Dwellings	A. Design	A. Laboratory	A. Volunteer work
B. Workplaces	B. Construction	B. Shop	
C. Recreation facilities	C. Assembly	C. Office/studio	B. Summer work
D. Toolmaking	D. Operation	D. Factory	
E. Vehicles	E. Repair	E. Government	C. Apprenticeships
F. Appliances	F. Reconstruction	F. Public organization	
G. Clothing	G. Creation/ innovation	G. Corporation	D. Entry-level work
H. Toys/ games	H. Manufacture	1. administration	
I. Electronics	I. Sales	2. work site	E. Semiskilled and skilled work
J. Computers	J. Advertising	3. retail outlet	
K. Communications	K. Fund-raising	4. sales office	F. Independent study
L. Machines	L. Regulation	H. Testing facility	
M. Printing	M. Law and contracts	I. Home	
	N. Education	J. College/university	

PROFILE FORM #5

18

Some Hints

on How

to Use

This Book

THE PROFILES in this book are designed to lead to action. They are meant to be used by youngsters for the actual exploration of vocation possibilities. They can be used by a young person without any assistance, or they can be used by parents and children together, or by school counselors and students, or by a group of friends. If you are a parent I suggest you read the whole book first and decide whether to share it with your daughter or son. Doing so might not be as simple as it sounds, since one implication of reading the book is that you might consider that there are sensible alternatives to going to college right after high school. Your child may not know that you are

. . . .

open to such alternatives and the question of what to do after high school may be a source of friction within the family. The offer to share the book can become tantamount to an admission that you are willing to sit down and discuss with your child alternatives to going straight from high school to college. There's no harm in making such an admission, and college will still be there for your child as a delaying action or a genuine choice involving vocational preference.

If you are about to graduate high school, or have just graduated and are thinking about work instead of college, you can read through and use the book yourself or share it with your parents. However, since it is essential to act on one's own behalf in the quest for personally meaningful work, I have addressed Parts Two and Three of this book, on the setup and use of profile forms, directly to the youngsters who will use them.

Concrete Ways
to Begin
the
Exploration
of Vocation

READ THROUGH the book before trying to work out a personal profile. Here are some suggestions about beginning a personal exploration of vocation:

1. Go back through the book, do some of the thought exercises, and fill out some sample profile forms. If you have already done them while reading, then go on to step 2, which starts you on your own personal exploration.

2. Set up bookshelf space specifically devoted to resources for the project. Begin with your diary, several notebooks, this book, and copies of the Yellow Pages of the telephone book of several cities. As you'll see, the Yellow Pages is one of the most useful sources of contacts you can find.

Ideally you should get your local Yellow Pages, the Yellow Pages of cities around you, and the Washington, D.C., and Manhattan volumes. You can usually get these free from the telephone company. Simply tell them the books are necessary resources for your work, which they are. There are also a number of general resources listed in the Appendix of this book, most of which are available at any public library or high school guidance office.

3. Set up a specific time each day to think about potential careers and keep informal notes of your thoughts. Use a notebook or diary specifically devoted to your quest for a vocation, and even give it a name if you want to. That's not any sillier than naming a guitar, a car, or a computer.

Begin by making a random list of work-related words that come to your mind during each thought session. Let yourself free-associate and don't be afraid to write down silly or even impossible things. Let yourself relax while you think about work. Your work diary is private, a sort of dream book dealing with lifelong possibilities. It might even help to visualize yourself doing work, or to imagine yourself twenty years from now, still caring about the work you chose and facing new challenges. You can generate a list as simple as:

- music: play, hear, listen, sell
- theater: act, produce, be famous and rich, own a theater
- biology: go to sea and watch the whales, protect the sea, find out about the bottom of the ocean

You can even write a story or draw pictures. The main thing is to feel your way into imagining things you might want to do if you had all of the choice in the world. Force yourself to do this every day for two weeks, and then continue to make entries on a regular basis and at the beginning and end of each week until you find a first job. At that point you might want to begin a diary of reflections on your work and use it to continue to discover ways to grow through meaningful work. Remember, it is a work diary, and therefore should be used to sort out the feelings and rewards of work from the other pressures you feel in your life. The intent is not to divide life and feelings about work into disconnected pieces. Rather, it is to help you settle into work that can be integrated into the rest of your life in a positive way.

As your exploration of vocation develops, your lists and imaginings can become more specific, or they can be reflective comments on the interviews you've had and the success or frustration you've experienced. It's helpful to keep a running account of your vocational journeying and reread it every once in a while. It's a way of keeping your dreams alive and having a chance to step back and see yourself develop.

Be sure to set up a ritual time to make entries in the diary or else it will be easy to put off thinking about vocation and eventually avoid the question altogether and let things happen to you. This might seem like a lot of effort, but it isn't much considering how many people let themselves fall into work they end up hating and how much of your life you spend working.

4. Another way to help clarify the quest for vocation is to find someone to talk to and work with in the development of a profile for yourself. You can choose a family member or a friend, someone who cares about your future. Some topics to talk about are:

- people you know who love their work
- people you know who hate their work
- people who are doing things you never expected they would end up doing
- people's dreams for their futures

Try to articulate as much as you can about these people.

Have these discussions on a regular basis, and if you decide to work on the profiles together, set up specific times to do it. Force yourself to keep to a schedule and devote yourself to trying to see how your dreams might play themselves out in the workplace.

Here are some ground rules for the discussion:

- Do not discuss private conflicts or disagreements. Do not bring the whole of family life or your love life into the discussion of vocation and career.
- No one may tell another what to do, or try to persuade, cajole, or trick someone into making a decision. The process must be open and honest to be effective and avoid making family or personal relations worse.
- No one may claim that they know what is best for someone else. On a positive level, show respect for people making decisions for themselves.
- Allow the conversations to explore many routes before either party makes a commitment to a specific program. Avoid premature decisions.
- Discuss finances openly and be clear that any promises made should be considered binding.
- Notes and notebooks are private and shared only by agreement.

After talking generally about vocation for a few sessions, make about ten copies each of the five profile forms in the book and put them in a folder.

Discuss the profile forms with your parents or friends, going through all five of them. It may seem boring and unnecessary, especially if you are certain that only one expresses your affinities. However, unexpected discoveries and affinities may arise, and it always makes sense to broaden the field of possibilities before making a choice that will lead to specific action. As the cyberneticist Heinz von Foerster said: "Always act in such a way as to broaden your choices." The wider the range of choices a person provides for herself or himself, the more likely that person is to find a fit between personal affinities and the world's possibilities.

There may be more than one profile form that suggests a career that interests you, and don't retreat from that complexity. Some people find or create work in areas that cross traditional vocational boundaries. For example, someone might want to design and construct recreational facilities for the handicapped with handicapped people. This cuts across WORK WITH PEOPLE and WORK WITH THINGS. Many creative activities involve integrating areas of work that are usually kept separate, also. The greater the fit between your inner affinities and the specifics of your profiles, the closer you might get to use your life in ways that are most fulfilling.

5. After a while, focus in on one type of work described by the profiles that seems interesting. Begin an elaborated profile and reach out to the community. Think of doing that kind of work in your mind. When you're in town, look for anything that might be relevant. If, when you're taking a walk, you notice a shop or library or business or some place that might provide resources for your quest, take a minute to stop and look around. Introduce yourself to people and tell them what you are looking for and ask for advice.

I remember asking a friend who was an inventor of valves and fasteners and other small but elegant and useful metal objects how she got her ideas. She said that the major sources of inspiration were variety stores, hardware stores, and department stores. Whenever she had a problem, such as designing a fastener that bound things at forty-seven degrees and had to be no bigger than three inches in each direction, she went to a place with lots of stuff for sale and let her mind run free. She found that she usually hit on some product that had nothing directly to do with her problem but that kindled an idea that she could use. This kind of indirect thinking is called "lateral thinking" by Edward DeBono, an expert on problem solving and creative thinking. You might want to look at his book of the same name during the course of your exploration. The book is useful for anyone who wants to develop creative solutions to perplexing problems.

Also use lateral strategies when you are looking for resources. Anything, any person, is a potential resource if you know how to look and ask. I've had wonderful discussions at bars and other social places about the widest range of topics and have found useful information in many casual conversations with strangers.

6. After you've gathered resources, prepare to contact people, visit places, and set up interviews.

7. After you've made contact with people, think through how you felt you presented yourself. Write your impressions down in your diary and discuss them. Don't look on a discouraging experience as a failure. Instead, take it as a learning experience, as training for the next interview.

Don't give up if you are shy or awkward or hesitant the first few times through. One way to get some confidence is to make a list of the questions you were asked in your first interviews and then, within the family, playact mock interviews and get accustomed to talking for yourself and about yourself. Being convincing in an interview is not a matter of talent so much as a matter of experience and sincerity.

8. Finally, it is a good idea to continue your diary as you begin to work and to continue to evaluate your work experiences. Ask people you work with about how they got their jobs and how they feel about what they are doing. Become a participant observer. Study the structure of the organization you work for, become knowledgeable about the social and economic effects of the work, of its financing, as well as of its social values. Also be alert to what you don't yet know and find out ways of increasing your knowledge.

How
to Research
a Profile
and
Use It

IT'S IMPOSSIBLE to examine all of the possible individual profiles that can be generated by the WORK WITH PEOPLE and other four profile forms that are given in this book. If you choose just one entry from each of the four columns in the forms, there are 4,284 possible WORK WITH PEOPLE profiles and 51,836 individual profiles that can be generated from the other forms—for a total of 56,120 simple profiles. There's no point in even trying to calculate or illustrate all possible complex profiles a teenager might formulate, nor any way to describe them in this book.

The specific nature of the research that you do is determined by the profile you choose and by the nature of the community you live in. Therefore, it makes sense to look at several specific elaborated profiles. Basically, however, they will all incorporate eleven steps, which we'll review in this chapter.

Before proceeding, I want to reiterate that the goal of using the profile forms is not merely to find a job. The program presented in this book tries to help teenagers focus on the substance and nature of work that interests them and might lead to a rewarding life. It assumes that young people have time to choose the form of their life's work and that time spent during the last years of high school and the year after high school can provide a firm foundation for future learning and work.

WORK WITH PEOPLE SAMPLE PROFILE 1: JANE

In order to test out the research strategy developed in this book I pretended to be a high school student, Jane, and used a profile that a friend of mine had filled out. I also pretended to be her parents and set out to research the possibilities for finding a way to explore the kind of work the profile pointed toward. The locale chosen for the experiment was Santa Rosa, California, a city of 120,000 about sixty miles north of San Francisco.

WORK WITH PEOPLE

Ages of People to Work With	Life Conditions of the People to Work With	Areas of Work	Ways You Can Become Involved
A. Infants	A. "Normal"	A. Social welfare	A. Volunteer work
		B. Education	
B. Early childhood (2 to 5)	B. Economically needy	C. Politics	B. Summer work
		D. Legal issues	
	C. At risk	E. Recreation	C. Apprenticeships
C. Young children (6 to 12)		F. Study of people	
	D. Mentally ill	G. Travel	D. Entry-level work
		H. Caring for others	
D. Teenagers	E. Physically ill	I. Medicine	E. Semiskilled and skilled work
		J. Nutrition and	
E. Grown-ups	F. Handicapped	food preparation	F. Independent study
		K. Transportation	
F. Seniors	G. Gifted	L. Public safety	
		M. Environment	
		N. Ergonomics	
		O. Communications and media	
		P. Organizing	
		Q. Arts	
		R. Sciences	

Jane's Profile

·

1 1 5

. . . .

I began by summarizing the profile in words and then tried to be more specific about the kind of things my pretend high school student wanted to do:

1. Summary of Profile

Work with handicapped senior citizens in the arts.

2. Elaboration of Profile

To work with mentally and perceptually handicapped (but not mentally disturbed) senior citizens in painting and drawing and other visual arts, and to take them on museum and other arts-related trips. The work could take place at a community center, convalescent home, or even in people's homes.

3. Gathering of Resources

Once the profile has been elaborated on, it is time to reach out and discover places where the kind of work described in the profile is done. It's better to start close to home and then, if necessary, move to larger cities. One way to start is to look through the Yellow Pages of the local phone book. Other ways are to contact people you know who already work in the field, or to go to a library and ask for reference books or journals that list organizations related to the kind of work you are interested in. For this profile, the fields of mental retardation, physical handicaps, and art therapy are relevant.

If nobody can help you with specific references, look in the *Guide to American Directories* or the *Encyclopedia of Associations*, both of which are in almost all libraries and list by category all of the organizations, firms, and advocacy groups in the United States that deal with specific issues or areas of work or charity. In this case you'd find seniors' organizations, handicapped organizations, and arts organizations all relevant to your research. Most groups listed are regional, statewide, or national, and so the best strategy is to find the groups closest to

.

home, contact them, and get referred to the best resources in your locale.

In the case of my research on this profile I didn't use the *Guide* or the *Encyclopedia*, but instead began with the index of the Yellow Pages of the Sonoma County telephone book and made a list of headings that related to work with handicapped seniors. Here are some of the listings that seemed possible: Senior Citizens, Physically Handicapped, Handicapped, Retardation, Mental Retardation, Therapy, Arts, Social Services Organizations. I chose Senior Citizens, and the illustration shows what I found listed under that heading.

Senior Citizens' Service Organizations

Cloverdale Senior Multi-Purpose Center
  201 Commercial Clvrdl 894 4826
Council On Aging Of Sonoma County
  Information & Referral
  Santa Rosa Ofc
    1000 Coddingtown Center 525 0143
  Paraguides 996 1411
  Senior Nutrition & Activities Program
    Cloverdale 100 King Clr Clvrdl . . 894 4172
  Forestville
    Center & Covey Rd Frstvl 887 1070
  Guerneville
    15010 Armstrong Woods Rd
    Gnvl 869 3998
  Healdsburg 133 Matheson Hbg . . 433 7515
  Santa Rosa Senior Center
    704 Bennett Valley Rd 545 6606
    Santa Rosa Home Delivered
    Meals 523 3244
  Silvercrest 1050 3d 544 3355

Council On Aging Of Sonoma County (Cont'd)
  Vintage House
    252 W Spain Snma 996 1414
    Windsor 9161 Starr Rd Wdsr . . . 838 9261
Petaluma People Services Center
  115 Liberty Pet 763 9866
Retired Senior Volunteer Program
  1041 4th 544 5993
RIVER COMMUNITY SERVICES SENIOR CENTER
  15010 Armstrong Woods Rd
  Gnvl **869 0618**
Santa Rosa Senior Center
  704 Bennett Valley Rd 545 8608
Santa Rosa Senior Day Services
  2000 Humboldt 546 4426
Senior Citizens Review 575 5570
Sonoma County Indian Health Project
  953 Sunset Av 527 5598
Sonoma Senior Day Services
  252 W Spain Snma 935 0850
Vintage House Senior Center
  252 W Spain Snma 996 0311

4. Choosing the First Lead to Pursue

Now comes the question of which of the organizations it makes sense to call first. Since you're beginning blind it doesn't make much difference which one you choose, though an educated guess about the most relevant listing can save time. The first few calls may lead nowhere, or the entry itself may lead to a dead end. Don't quit—this is just the beginning of the quest. Also tell everyone you call what you're looking for and ask them if they might have suggestions. People are often quite generous in sharing their resources. Build up a list of as many contacts as you can.

It might be a good idea, as a first phone call, to try an organization whose name implies it is an umbrella group that has contacts with other organizations in the field. In my case, the first phone book entry, Council on Aging of Sonoma County, seemed to have that characteristic. I decided to call it first.

5. Planning the First Inquiry

Before making the call, it's a good idea to write down notes on how you will introduce the purpose of your call, as well as make a list of questions you would like to ask. Before phoning, prepare what you'll say. It makes sense to rehearse the phone call with a friend. Be clear about what information you're seeking and don't forget to set up an appointment. Personal introductions don't have to be formal or complex but should minimally include:

- the caller's name
- the school attending or attended
- the purpose of the call
- an opening for future contacts or an interview or visit

For this particular call I made these notes:

Purpose of Jane's Call and List of Information to Give and Questions to Ask

A. The purpose of the call is to discover whether there is any way young people can become involved in working with senior citizens who are physically or mentally handicapped, teaching them painting or drawing or other forms of graphic arts, or taking them on art trips.
   1. Does it make a difference where the work takes place?
   2. Can the work be voluntary or for pay (entry level)?

B. Information to give
1. Current school status
2. Amount of time to be given (length of time, hours per week)
3. Skills: painting, drawing, etc.
4. Resources to be provided: a driver's license, an insured car for trips
C. Questions to ask
1. Is there any training required?
2. How specifically does one follow up on the call (who to talk to next, how to get an interview, where to visit, etc.)?

6. First Inquiry and Response

Call Number 1: I called the Council on Aging and explained to the woman who answered that I counseled high school students who wanted to delay college and spend the year after high school exploring career possibilities. One of the students, I continued, wanted to find a way to use her skills as an artist to work with handicapped senior citizens. I was assured that there must be some way to set that up but that the Council on Aging did not deal with specific program placement. The woman I spoke to suggested I call the Santa Rosa Senior Center and the Santa Rosa Community Center and gave me their phone numbers.

Call Number 2: I pursued these suggestions and called the Senior Center first and explained the nature of my request. I was put through to the director of the center, who informed me that the center had a choral group, a drama club, and painting classes. Most of the classes were for handicapped and nonhandicapped seniors together, though some sections of the classes were for the more seriously handicapped who required special attention. The center welcomed volunteers and had an ongoing interviewing process. People could volunteer at any time during the year and begin work soon after the interview if everything was satisfactory. In addition, the center welcomed proposals for new volunteer classes and provided orientation sessions for new volunteers. High school students and recent graduates were very welcome. The youngster I was talking about was welcome to visit and get a tour any time she liked. And it would be good if she could call the center herself.

Call Number 3: I decided to call the Community Center as well, and talked to the director. She told me she began as a volunteer at the center, then got a part-time job, and recently was appointed director. Her center had specific programs for handicapped seniors, welcomed new programs, and needed volunteers all the time. She also added that she liked to help young people who volunteered and give them a sense of career opportunities in social and recreational work with seniors and the handicapped. Interviews were also conducted on an ongoing basis at the Community Center.

I then asked about the possibility of getting an entry-level job working with handicapped seniors, and she said that there were a number of private seniors' communities and convalescent homes that hired youngsters to work in recreation and the arts and she gave me the names of a half dozen of them. She also suggested I talk to the YMCA, and said she'd send me information on other organizations' programs as well as those at her center. I got the information in the mail the next day.

7. Preparation for Follow-up

Before going to an interview or making a visit, make certain preparations. Be sure to have a résumé, a number of references, and a short descriptive essay on your skills and experiences and why you want to do a particular type of work.

In addition, think about how to present yourself and be clear on how dress, language, gesture, and attitude affect the interviewer. It is usual to leave a copy of your résumé and references with the interviewer. The essay is also a good thing to share.

. . . .

A. Résumé

A résumé is, just as it implies, a summary of a life's work and experience. Some people are shy about putting down their experiences and often underestimate what they have done. Don't underestimate yourself. Things you've done that you feel are ordinary and unimportant may be significant to a potential employer.

Be sure, when you write a résumé, to list all of the things you have done in your community and school, as well as your hobbies and the out-of-school groups you belong to. Also make sure that everything that you do or know that relates to the work you want is included on the résumé.

On the two following pages are one usual form of résumé that can be used and a sample filled-out résumé.

B. References

References are very important to prospective employers or people in charge of apprenticeship or learning programs. The people you ask should be picked carefully. It is important that people who give references know you, like you, have seen you do a number of different things, and can speak of you from experience. The following types of people are very good sources of references: doctors, teachers, former or present employers, ministers, camp counselors, community leaders, people you have done volunteer or community work with, people who have given you music or art lessons. You should have at least three references, and not more than five.

You may ask people for written references, but it is most typical simply to ask people to let you use their name. Append to your résumé a sheet with your name and address and the list of your references.

C. Essay

This should be a one-page essay on the things you have enjoyed doing, on what you would like to do, and on your feel-

Résumé

Name
Address
Telephone Number

<u>Position Desired</u>   [Description]

<u>Education</u>   [In this section educational experience is listed
from the present back. Do not hesitate to include
music lessons, camps, and any other type of
learning!]

<u>Experience</u>   [List jobs, extra curricular activities, travel,
community service, groups such as church groups,
Scouts, volunteer work, student council,
athletics, school clubs, performances, exhibits.
Don't be shy!]

<u>Awards</u>   [List school or community awards, art shows,
medals, certificates.]

<u>Interests</u>   [List hobbies, skills, collections — anything
that makes you an interesting person and tells
something about what you are like.]

Résumé Form

Résumé

Jane Roman
1414 J Street
Rogers, IL 43444
706-889-0001

<u>Position Desired</u>   Work with handicapped senior
citizens in the area of the
arts

<u>Education</u>
1985 to present   Valley South High School
Summer 1987   Rogers Music Camp
Summer 1986   Study abroad: Greece

<u>Experience</u>
1986 to present   Reading tutor in ABC program
1985 to present   Volunteer, Community Cleanup
Group
1983 to present   Drama Club (6 performances)
1983 to present   Art Club, Exhibit Director

<u>Awards</u>
1987   Honorable Mention, Painting,
Community Center Art Show

<u>Interests</u>   Painting, theater, travel,
helping handicapped people

Sample Résumé

1 2 3

ings about the future. Here are a few sample paragraphs from such essays:

> I always liked to paint and draw and began art lessons when I was twelve. Most of my work has been studies of faces of young children and very old people in different moods. When I was fifteen I won an award for one of these portraits. I want to continue painting and want to teach other people how to paint too.

> My grandfather lived in an old-age home before he died. I used to visit him two times a week and read to him for hours. He loved books but his eyes were very bad and he could no longer read. Other people at the home liked my reading and so I read to a whole group of people after a while. Then the old people began telling me stories. I wrote some of them down and made some booklets on the lives of old people with the community oral history project. In the future I think I would like to work with old people and also become involved with putting books together and publishing them.

D. Personal Letter of Introduction

Sometimes you will be asked to submit a personal letter of introduction in writing before your interview. In those cases it is also typical for a prospective employer to request a copy of your résumé, your references, and possibly your essay as well. Having this material enables the interviewer to prepare appropriate questions for you and is not a sign of rejection or lack of confidence.

Here is a personal letter of introduction that I wrote:

Dear Ms. Gold,

(i)   I am writing to inquire about the possibility of doing volunteer work at the Santa Rosa Senior Center. I am a high school senior and am currently exploring the possibility of pursuing a career working with handicapped senior citizens. I would like to have some practical experience in that field this summer or next year and understand you have programs that might provide this experience.

(ii)   During my high school years I have been very interested in the arts and have exhibited a number of my pastels and watercolors at local amateur shows. I have also worked in other visual arts media, and would like to combine my experience in the arts with work with seniors.

(iii)   My interest in working with senior citizens is derived from time I spent painting and talking with my grandmother. She spent the last years of her life in a rest home and was not very happy there. I would like to do something to make older people feel more wanted and provide them with activities (such as painting and drawing) that could give them pleasure.

(iv)   I'm enclosing a copy of my résumé and a list of references as you requested. I look forward to hearing from you about a date for an interview. Thank you for your interest and attention.

                Sincerely,

This letter has four paragraphs, which are about all you need for a personal letter of introduction. Here is a general outline for the content of these paragraphs:

   i. why you are writing and what you would like to do
  ii. your skills or experience, especially things that relate to the work you are seeking
 iii. your reason for being interested in this kind of work
 iv. a request for an interview, a note about enclosures in your letter, and a thank-you

E. Presentation of Self

The way you present yourself to a prospective employer, or to someone whose work you are interested in, is very important. There are a few absolute no-no's:

- Never chew gum or smoke in an interview.
- Don't curse or in any way show off your ability to be outrageous.
- Don't wear your worst clothes.
- Don't be late.

Given these minimal caveats, it's best to dress comfortably, be yourself, and not try to take on the dress or manners that you think someone else will like just for the sake of an interview. Try your best to be at ease and natural. Visualize yourself as someone you would like to meet and talk to. Imagine yourself to be the interviewer and think of the kind of person you would like to hire to work with you.

8. Interviews and Visits

I didn't pursue the next logical steps, which would be to make visits to the two centers, call the rest homes, and decide after the visits whether any of them provided the kind of environment I felt would provide a good work and learning experience. However, I did give the information to some youngsters who lived in Santa Rosa, and one of them became a volunteer teacher in an aerobics class for handicapped adults.

9. Placements and Evaluation of the Working Situation

After the interview there is always the possibility of being offered a position as a volunteer, apprentice, or worker. It makes sense to pursue several options at the same time. Unless the first thing you are offered is exactly what you want, waiting and trying several places is a sensible strategy. Another sensible thing to do is check out the reliability and reputation of any place that offers you a position. This is particularly important if you might have to move to another city or even country to pursue your quest for meaningful work. In fact, if you are thinking of working away from home it is essential to check out places where you might work before going to an interview.

Here are some suggestions for questions to ask and things to research about potential workplaces:

- Find out how many years the business or organization has been operating. Also find out about the experience of the people who will supervise you. You can do this by asking or by consulting a local Better Business Bureau, which

will also tell you whether the place has any pending complaints against it.

- Try to talk to other workers and people who have been
  clients about the nature of the organization before
  accepting a job offer.
- What kind of employee insurance does the workplace
  carry? Are volunteers and apprentices covered by that
  insurance? You need that insurance and you must be sure
  that you have no liability for any accidents that might
  happen at the workplace. This is particularly important
  when you are working with people, especially those that
  have handicaps. You need to be protected in a reasonable
  way.

10. Supplementary Learning and Work

While looking for the right place to work or volunteer, a
few other things have to be considered about the year after
high school. One of them is where the money will come from.
It's easiest if you live at home or get living expenses from your
parents. It's also possible to get a part-time job in order to support volunteer work if that's the only way you can find to get
into the career you want. Sometimes you can find a paying
apprenticeship or an entry-level job that will support you.

For some, it's worth using the resources you might have
had available to you if you had gone to college to find out about
how you want to spend your working life. Certainly it's a case
worth making with your parents.

Another thing to consider is supplementary part-time
learning that can enrich work during that year of exploration.
For example, the hypothetical youngster in the profile might
want to take an art class and a class on an introduction to problems of the handicapped given by the local junior college. Or
she might want to attend training sessions at the Council on
Aging, or contact national organizations for the handicapped
and attend regional meetings. She might also look into art therapy and take training classes in that field as well. It's important
to build as rich a learning program as possible around the exploration of potential life's work.

. . . .

11. Program and Expectations for the Year

Here are some suggestions of things to add to your vocational diary: Write out a description of the program that emerges from the research and outreach you do, and keep a record of the nature of the work and supplementary learning that you finally settle on. This would include a job description, perhaps an informal description of the place of work and the people encountered there.

Finally, before actually beginning work, make a list of expectations for the coming summer or year's work. You can use it as a guide to check whether the original intent of taking time off to explore career and vocation is working. If you discover, early enough, that things aren't working out as you'd hoped, you'll have time to change your program and find a better placement.

Here are some possible expectations for the profile we've been considering:

- to learn about the physical coordination of handicapped seniors so that my art programs do not frustrate them (for example, what kinds of brushes are best, how the colors should be mixed, who does cleanup)
- to discover if I have the patience for all-day work with seniors
- to be able to list the rewards I get from the work
- to discover different ways of working with seniors that lead to decently paying jobs
- to find out about what additional training I might need

SUMMARY OF RESEARCH AND INTERVIEW PLAN

Here is a summary of the steps, from profile form to interviews and work, that were described above. The list provides a general framework that should be useful for pursuing specific plans for summer work or the year after high school. It makes sense

· · · · · · · · · · · · · · ·

to get a notebook and record what you do with the profile and what responses you get.

Profile Checklist

1. Summary of Profile
2. Elaboration of Profile
3. Gathering of Resources
4. Choosing the First Lead to Pursue
5. Planning the First Inquiry
6. First Inquiry and Response: Call Number 1 (if necessary, Call Number 2, Call Number 3, etc.)
7. Preparation for Follow-up
   A. Résumé
   B. References
   C. Essay
   D. Personal letter of introduction
   E. Presentation of self
8. Interviews and Visits
9. Placements and Evaluation of the Working Situation
10. Supplementary Learning and Work
11. Program and Expectations for the Year

WORK WITH PEOPLE SAMPLE PROFILE 2: RAPHAEL

Raphael had an acute episode of rheumatic fever when he was a child. He was bedridden for a while and has never forgotten how kind people were to him during those despairing days when there was a chance he might have suffered permanent heart damage. In particular he remembers Stuart, a teenager his parents hired to play chess, build models, and do puzzles with him. Stuart spent three hours a day taking care of Raphael, an only child, who felt as if he had an older brother in Stuart. Raphael decided that when he was older he would find a way to do some work with children who had serious illnesses. When he was a junior in high school his father suggested he take a

·

year before going to college to explore ways to realize his childhood dream. I asked them to try the profile and research strategies I was developing. Here are the results:

WORK WITH PEOPLE

Ages of People to Work With	Life Conditions of the People to Work With	Areas of Work	Ways You Can Become Involved
A. Infants	A. "Normal"	A. Social welfare	A. Volunteer work
		B. Education	
B. Early childhood (2 to 5)	B. Economically needy	C. Politics	B. Summer work
		D. Legal issues	
	C. At risk	E. Recreation	C. Apprenticeships
C. Young children (6 to 12)		F. Study of people	
	D. Mentally ill	G. Travel	D. Entry-level work
		H. Caring for others	
D. Teenagers	E. Physically ill	I. Medicine	E. Semiskilled and skilled work
		J. Nutrition and	
E. Grown-ups	F. Handicapped	food preparation	F. Independent study
		K. Transportation	
F. Seniors	G. Gifted	L. Public safety	
		M. Environment	
		N. Ergonomics	
		O. Communications and media	
		P. Organizing	
		Q. Arts	
		R. Sciences	

Raphael's Profile

1. Summary of Profile

My goal is work in the areas of recreation and caring with six- to twelve-year-old (give or take a year or two) children suffering from serious illnesses. I want to work or volunteer during the summer.

2. Elaboration of Profile

By serious illness is meant an illness that happens during life, not one that is inherited. It is hoped that such illness is temporary, though it causes an immediate crisis in a child's life.

By caring I mean working to keep the child happy, being available to talk about frustrations, loneliness, and how to deal with pain. Psychology or social work might be the field. By recreation I mean doing crafts, exercising, taking walks, playing games, doing arts and crafts.

3. Gathering of Resources

A. My doctor and pediatrician
B. Yellow Pages listings: hospitals, social service organizations, physicians, psychologists, recreation, home health services

4. Choosing the First Lead to Pursue

Our family doctor

5. Planning the First Inquiry

A. The purpose of the call is to find out if there is any way to volunteer or apprentice at a hospital or other medical facility that serves ill children and where one can learn about needs of the ill.
B. Information to give
   1. High school experience
   2. Reason for wanting to do this work
   3. Skills: games, puzzles, models, physical skills in playground games
C. Questions to ask
   1. Is there a career in this kind of work?
   2. What kind of long-range training does it require?
   3. What does it make sense to study or what skills should one master?

6. First Inquiry and Response

Call Number 1: The family's doctor says he has occasional need for someone to take care of an ill child at home, but it is a very irregular thing, not one to plan a program around. However, there are many caring professions for the ill, including social work, child psychology, nursing (pediatric nursing in particular). He said that local junior college has decent introductory courses in all of these subjects, and suggested that a call be made to local hospital volunteer organizations or to social service organizations.

Call Number 2: Yellow Pages listing: Volunteer Center of Sonoma County. Talked to assistant director, who said they had dozens of volunteer programs throughout the county and helped people set up programs as well. They could find a placement, maybe even see if some sort of apprenticeship could be arranged. The first step would be to come and look through their files and get an informal interview. The interview could be set up at any time. They also suggested I call Social Advocates for Youth.

Call Number 3: As suggested by the Volunteer Center, I called Social Advocates for Youth. They have programs in substance dependency counseling, drug addiction, and youth employment. They said to come around and visit but didn't think they had what I wanted.

Call Number 4: Called children's wing of County Hospital, volunteer services, and they said they always needed volunteers to work with children on the wards and suggested I visit and come for an interview. Think I'll do two interviews before making additional phone calls.

7. Preparation for Follow-up

A. Résumé (see opposite)

B. References

- Family doctor
- English teacher
- Computer and chess club supervisor
- Sunday School director

Résumé

Raphael Stone
1214 Julian Drive
Rosemount, CA 45678
707-882-8001

<u>Position Desired</u>   Work caring for and assisting
                 seriously ill children ages
                 six to twelve

<u>Education</u>
1985 to present   Valley South High School
Summer 1987   Computer Program, North
                      Junior College
Summer 1986   Animation Class, North Junior
                      College
Summer 1985   Rogers Computer Camp
1982 to 1985   J. Frost Junior High School

<u>Experience</u>
1986 to present   High School Student Council
1985 to present   Chair, High School Community
                      Volunteers
1985 to present   Chess Club, Computer Club
1983 to present   Part-time work at Safeway,
                      Lucky

<u>Awards</u>
1987   Elks High School Service
                      Award
                   First Place, H.S, Chess
                      Tournament
                   Atari Connection Software
                      Award

<u>Interests</u>   Chess, computers, crafts and
                   games, helping young people

Raphael's Résumé

.
1 3 3

C. Essay

I am a senior at Valley South High School and during this year have been working with the student council developing community service programs for high school students. We have managed to get CPR training at our school and have students volunteer in the state park and in two local community centers. In addition to this work I have been involved in the chess and computer clubs, and have done volunteer work at a local hospice through my church's education program.

I am a fairly good student and like to learn things I can share with other people. At this time I am thinking about working with children who are suffering from some kind of serious illness. I had rheumatic fever when I was young and a teenager took care of me and helped me at the worst moments in my life. He made me feel that it must be wonderful to help others. This might lead to my becoming a psychologist, a recreation therapist, or maybe even a pediatric nurse. I hope to spend next year exploring these vocational options.

[Note how well Raphael worked the suggestions he got from his doctor into his essay.]

D. Presentation of Self

Feel comfortable with myself.

8. Interviews and Visits

Volunteer Center

I had a long talk with the assistant director, who said the résumé, references, and essay weren't necessary but made her job much easier. I went through the cards and found a program for convalescing children, mostly with broken bones and other physical traumas, which I hadn't thought about before but might be interesting. I also found several requests for doing home visits associated with a meals-on-wheels program. There's a lot that is possible here. The assistant director said she thought something could be worked out on a test basis for the summer and it might lead to something more substantial if

I decided to make a long-term commitment. I agreed to call back within a week.

County Hospital

The volunteer services director took me for a tour of the wards. There are some playrooms and physical therapy gyms. Also the hospital has a puppet show program and a number of arts programs and the director of volunteers expressed interest in developing a computer program and a chess group of ten- to fifteen-year-olds. I met and talked with an interested pediatric nurse (an RN), and she seemed to love her work. I promised to call back within a week.

9. Placements and Evaluation of the Working Situation

I am about to call back. I think I'd like to start at the hospital because there are professionals there I might learn from. I can also see what kind of work they do and maybe get to help them. I should thank the Volunteer Center organization and tell them that I will probably be volunteering at County Hospital.

10. Supplementary Learning and Work

I got a catalog from Rosemont Junior College and found that there are summer school and night classes called "Arts, Crafts, and Sciences for Children," "Development Stages of Childhood," and "Fundamentals of Clinical Nursing." For the nursing class a CPR card is required so I should get that first. Maybe the best thing is to get the CPR card and take the arts and crafts class while volunteering this summer and do the other classes in the fall. I also have to find a part-time job—Taco Bell, here I come.

11. Program and Expectations for the Year

Summer: Volunteer at hospital, take CPR and arts and crafts class, work part-time

Fall: Continue at hospital and look for apprentice position, take nursing and child-development classes

Expectations:

- to see if I enjoy spending time with children who have serious illnesses and feel it is a good thing for me to be doing
- to discover whether I have something to offer them
- to find out the way different people (doctors, nurses, physical therapists, etc.) work with children who are ill or injured
- to see if I want to work with older children as well
- to get a feel for what college can offer me if I choose to do this sort of work
- to keep my work diary going and add some pictures and descriptions of the people I work with

Raphael volunteered for a summer at the county hospital and was hired as an orderly that September. In February he decided that hospital work was right for him, and on the advice of one of the RNs, he enrolled in the local junior college in a recreational-therapy program. He's been told that the hospital will keep him on and probably promote him on graduation from the two-year junior-college program.

. . . .

Questions
to Ask
Yourself
When You Read
Through
the Profiles

AS YOU read through the detailed descriptions of the profiles analyzed in Part Three of this book ask yourself the following questions. These questions might help you focus on your own affinities for one form of work or another and provide you with a portrait of the kind of worker you would like to be.

QUESTIONS ABOUT YOUR CO-WORKERS

These questions are designed to help you focus on the personal environments you are likely to encounter in a particular form of work. They should help you develop a sense of the level of sociability that you would be comfortable living with five days a week. For example, if you choose to do environmental work monitoring the ozone layer in a remote part of the Antarctic it is likely that your closest friends will be penguins and other birds. On the other hand, if you work in a classroom you'll be in the constant presence of at least twenty young people for five hours a day; if you do survey work you'll be in contact with hundreds of people but only on the most casual of levels.

Here are questions to be raised with respect to the entries in the profile forms:

- How many people will I be encountering on a regular basis in this work? How many do I feel comfortable and natural with?
- Will I have bosses and will my ideas be heard? Do I want to work under close supervision or do I want to be my own boss? What middle ground can I live with?
- Does this work involve meeting new people all of the time and being on public display? Do I want this?
- Will I have to supervise other people or be responsible for the health and safety of others? Are these responsibilities I want to assume?
- Will the people I work with have the same ideas and style as I do or at least as I feel comfortable with? How much tolerance do I have for people who think, dress, and behave differently? Will I stand out as different in this job and will it bother me?

QUESTIONS ABOUT THE PHYSICAL DEMANDS OF THE WORK

Some jobs require moving around, and others sitting down; some involve small motor skills such as assembling electronic devices, and others large motor skills such as swimming and erecting steel sculptures. Since full-time work is just that, it's important to be physically comfortable in your life's work.

·

Here are physical things to consider when you read through the profile forms:

- What specific physical demands are made by this kind of work?
- Can I stand to do this kind of physical work? For example, do I want to sit for six hours a day, or work at a computer screen, or be constantly moving around or working at peak energy level?
- What kinds of dexterity and skill are required by this type of work and am I interested in acquiring them?
- Does this job require much traveling? How well do I travel? Do I enjoy it?
- Are there health and safety conditions that have to be considered· in this form of work? Do I have any limiting physical conditions that might make this kind of work unnecessarily burdensome? For example, if I have asthma, will I be able to do this form of work?

QUESTIONS ABOUT THE WORK ENVIRONMENT

- For the career described in some part of a profile form, what is the nature of the workplace? Is it indoors or outdoors, changing or static, small or cavernous, noisy or silent, light or dark? Is the entire environment the same or are there variations that workers experience over the course of a day or week?
- Considering the oppositions in the first question, what kind of work environment do I feel most comfortable with? And what kind might drive me crazy?
- What control might I have over my physical work environment?
- What tools do I have to use in this kind of work? How do I feel about the tools: Do I feel easy or uneasy about having to master them? (This question is particularly important when you are considering work such as blowing glass

or erecting a steel sculpture or fine-tuning an engine or making telescopic or microscopic observations.)
- How much of this kind of work can still be done if I become physically ill? How much are the skills I'll acquire transferable to other modes of work?

QUESTIONS ABOUT THE PSYCHOLOGICAL NATURE OF WORK

- What level of stress is involved in this work? Is it continuous, as in emergency fire control work, or intermittent, as in design projects or human and animal observation?
- What is the nature of the rewards in the work? Are they continuous or do they come at the end of a project? Are they internal and personal or are they collective? Do they come from above, from clients, from co-workers, or from the work itself?
- Is there occasion for intimacy? For privacy? How psychically close are people who do this kind of job to each other? How does the job relate to the larger communities it serves or affects?
- Is occasional boredom unavoidable in this kind of work? Or is there continual and perhaps exhausting stimulation? What balance between calm and stimulation do I function best with?
- Is continuing learning and growth part of this work? Can I expand my knowledge and understanding through it or is there a tendency toward stagnation that comes with years of doing the work? How much do I need to learn new things and acquire new skills? Would I rather perfect some skills or develop new ones and accept a decent level of mastery of others?

These twenty questions should help you form a profile of yourself as a worker. It would be too tedious to ask each of the questions of each of the categories in the profile forms. However, keep them in the back of your mind as you read through the profiles' components. When you finally choose a profile to elaborate upon and a career to try, go back to these questions and answer them for yourself in pretty specific ways. They can help you test the strength of your affinities for a certain kind of work.

It might also help to sketch a personal profile for yourself as a worker and, after a year or two, come back to it to see whether the nature of your work fits your nature as a worker.

part three

. . . .

A Description and Analysis of the Profiles

. . . .

Profile Form 1:

WORK

WITH

PEOPLE

WORK WITH PEOPLE

Ages of People to Work With	Life Conditions of the People to Work With	Areas of Work	Ways You Can Become Involved
A. Infants	A. "Normal"	A. Social welfare	A. Volunteer work
		B. Education	
B. Early childhood (2 to 5)	B. Economically needy	C. Politics	B. Summer work
		D. Legal issues	
	C. At risk	E. Recreation	C. Apprenticeships
C. Young children (6 to 12)		F. Study of people	
	D. Mentally ill	G. Travel	D. Entry-level work
D. Teenagers		H. Caring for others	
	E. Physically ill	I. Medicine	E. Semiskilled and skilled work
E. Grown-ups		J. Nutrition and food preparation	
	F. Handicapped	K. Transportation	F. Independent study
F. Seniors		L. Public safety	
	G. Gifted	M. Environment	
		N. Ergonomics	
		O. Communications and media	
		P. Organizing	
		Q. Arts	
		R. Sciences	

RALPH'S CHOICE AND THE DEVELOPMENT OF A PROFILE

Ralph, one of the youngsters I've been counseling, told me he would like to work with people but he knew he didn't want to be a teacher or a doctor, and asked me whether there were other ways to accomplish his goal. His question set me thinking about people working with people, about the range and variety of services people provide to other people in our society. I came up with a taxonomy of people services and put it into a profile form (Profile Form #1), which I shared with Ralph. I tried to include the kind of people Ralph might work with, the services he could provide, and the ways he could become involved. The taxonomy is not meant to be all-inclusive and if you can think of any additions please include them in your profile. As with all of the taxonomies in this book, it is based on a lot of thought, reading, and analysis, but it does not make any claim at being exhaustive or the only way to go about codifying aspects of working with people.

Ralph and I went through the form together, talked about each of the categories (which I will elaborate on below), and came up with a profile of his preferences. He said he had always wanted to work with babies, and that he had a desire to work with people in serious medical trouble. He also said that he wanted to care for people, not as a doctor but more as a nurse even though nursing had the aura of being "woman's work." He had a whole summer available and was willing to volunteer somewhere or accept minimal pay just to test himself out. He was also willing to spend a year after high school working with people if he could get minimum wage, or even wash dishes or wait tables at night and volunteer his services during the day. We came up with the profile shown on the next page.

Ralph indicated that developing a profile helped him articulate to his parents and friends his secret wishes about work. He had been afraid to share them with anyone before, much less actually try out the work.

Once Ralph developed a profile of his preferences, the next step was to find out who worked with infants who had serious

. . . .

WORK WITH PEOPLE

Ages of People to Work With	Life Conditions of the People to Work With	Areas of Work	Ways You Can Become Involved
A. Infants	A. "Normal"	A. Social welfare B. Education	A. Volunteer work
B. Early childhood (2 to 5)	B. Economically needy	C. Politics D. Legal issues	B. Summer work
C. Young children (6 to 12)	C. At risk	E. Recreation F. Study of people	C. Apprenticeships
	D. Mentally ill	G. Travel	D. Entry-level work
D. Teenagers	E. Physically ill	H. Caring for others I. Medicine	E. Semiskilled and skilled work
E. Grown-ups	F. Handicapped	J. Nutrition and food preparation	F. Independent study
F. Seniors	G. Gifted	K. Transportation L. Public safety M. Environment N. Ergonomics O. Communications and media P. Organizing Q. Arts R. Sciences	

Ralph's Profile

medical problems, and what were the ways in which Ralph could be of use to them as a caring person. A local hospital had an intensive-care unit for babies, and as it turned out was always in need of volunteeers to do very simple things such as get coffee for the doctors and nurses and on occasion monitor some of the computer screens that kept track of the babies' conditions. They also needed people to play with and feed recovering babies and small children in the hospital's nursery. Ralph volunteered for a summer and then was hired as a part-time aide for a year. Fortunately, his parents could support him so he lived at home and was able to pay for his own needs and contribute to food costs with the little he earned at the hospital supplemented by a part-time job at a fast-food chain.

The work Ralph does is routine, simple, and yet so rewarding that he is now considering entering a nursing program. For him, each patient presents new challenges and rewards. Nursing would not be a bad choice for him as there is an enormous shortage of LPNs and RNs throughout the country, and the pay is reasonable.

I believe it was smart of Ralph to begin to work with seriously ill infants on a tentative basis rather than enter a formal program. He needs to know how he will respond to that work's demands before committing years of his life to training and a profession.

THE WORK WITH PEOPLE PROFILE

The four major categories in the WORK WITH PEOPLE taxonomy are:

1. the ages of people you might like to work with
2. the social, psychological, economic, and medical conditions of people's lives
3. the areas you can work in
4. the ways in which you can become involved

Ages

It's important for those who might like to work with people to think through what personal rewards they want from their work. They should also consider what kind of people they feel comfortable spending time with. A while ago a friend of mine became a kindergarten teacher. She had the most miserable time during her first year teaching and once, over a beer, she told me that she was frustrated with her students because she couldn't talk to them about politics, economics, history, and civil rights. I reminded her that she was working with five-year-olds who had other things on their minds, and suggested she teach junior high school or high school. The next year she transferred to a junior high where she taught social studies and was a wonderful and quite happy teacher. The kindergarten children were not giving her the rewards she needed in order to put energy and love into her work, whereas the junior high students engaged her intelligence and emotions in ways that energized her. She found her place working with people in junior high school. Sometimes you have to experiment working in different contexts before finding work that is rewarding to you. It's important not to give up if your first work experience doesn't meet your expectations or fulfill your dreams.

I began my teaching career working with severely disturbed children who made little or no progress over the course of a year and whose pain was unbearable to me. As much as I wanted to teach, these students made me uncomfortable and impatient, and I realized that working with the disturbed was not for me. After a year I decided to work in a public school with normal and somewhat wild children where I felt perfectly at home.

My wife, Judy, however, found teaching thirty children in the confines of a classroom suffocating and exasperating and only lasted in the New York City public schools for a few months. But she became an excellent teacher of severely disturbed children and had the patience and love necessary to be useful to her students.

You have to match your affinities and needs to the work you choose to do. Some people do good work with older, institutionalized adults, while others simply cannot survive in that context. Some can work with infants, while others get nauseous changing diapers. Some people want to nurse, others to teach, counsel, or play. The following taxonomy of people-related work can be used as a projective test to help young people decide whether working with people is something they would like to do. Each of the categories should be explored separately and then a profile of potential work possibilities, some samples of which will be described, can be assembled.

Of course, during the course of one's life, preferences might change. Some people might like to work with older people when they are young and with infants when they get older, or might like to work with youths when they're in their twenties and with middle-aged people when they achieve middle age. I've noticed, for example, that teachers frequently choose to work with students the same age as their own children and when given the choice will move up in grade level as their own children grow older.

It is not necessary to make a work choice that is binding for one's whole life, but it is important to determine where you want to begin.

A. Infants

Working with babies requires patience, gentleness, playfulness, a delight in holding and touching an infant, and a willingness to change diapers and clean up messes. Some people take delight in the presence of new life, but many of us prefer to talk to children, run around and play with them. Infants don't do those things yet. They cry and laugh in ways many adults who are not in daily contact with babies forget. And they throw tantrums, have trouble getting to sleep, and can't directly express their needs. You have to be attuned to the nuances of baby language and take pleasure in the small ways you can nurture babies in order to make a career of working with infants. And you have to be confident enough to hold them and rock them and carry them around.

Baby-sitting is one way to get experience with infants. Another way, of course, is having baby brothers or sisters, and helping feed, clothe, and change them. However, many teenagers have no direct experience caring for infants. There are volunteer services at hospitals and social service agencies that can provide this experience for youngsters who feel they might like to work with infants, and a few summers of volunteer work during high school can give one a sense of whether working with infants is right.

In addition, many working parents need help with their babies and it is possible to set up a small baby-care business or work at a child-care center right after high school. Some infant care is provided by corporations, and there are jobs available for people without experience but with the patience and calmness needed to work with infants. However, infant care has many other aspects, ranging from emergency care in hospitals to designing or selling toys and clothes for infants. One can eventually choose to become a pediatrician, a developmental

. . . .

psychologist, an infant advocate lawyer, a toy or clothes designer, or perhaps a welfare caseworker or infant/parent counselor in a social service agency. What is important for young people who might like to work with infants is to have some experience working with them and test out affinities for that type of work.

B. Early Childhood (2 to 5)

Children two to five years old explode into the world. The development of will is perhaps most characteristic of children this age. They want all the power of adults and don't quite have the bodies and coordination to wield it, nor do they understand the consequences of some of their actions. They don't quite understand boiling water, the blood that leaks out of their bodies when they get cut, or the power of electricity in a socket. Yet two-to-five-year-olds can be a delight. They play with language as they learn it, ask the most impertinent and delightful questions, and make friends for the first time. If one has the endurance, spending time with two-to-five-year-olds can be like rediscovering what it was like to see the world for the first time.

Working with children from the ages of two to five is, according to many people, a "growth industry." With the growth of the number of women working and the increase in single-parent families, child care and early-childhood education are expanding. There is work in play groups, child-care centers, foster homes, summer camps, child group homes, schools, as well as au pair jobs, all of which are available to youngsters out of high school. There is also work in providing nutrition, clothing, and shelter for children from poor families, as well as opportunities in recreation and entertainment.

C. Young Children (6 to 12)

Six-year-olds can seem amazingly mature, and twelve-year-olds are quite mature. Working with children in this age range requires a delight in language, in talking with children, and in playing physical and intellectual games with them. This age, in my experience, is when children's personal identity and self-

.

1 5 1

awareness develop and when their role in a society of friends becomes clarified. It is a time of jealousies and friendships, of reaching out beyond the family and looking up to teenagers for style and advice. It's fun to work with children this age if you're full of energy, are willing to be silly on occasion and intimate and compassionate on others.

Children from six to twelve spend a good part of their lives in the organized atmosphere of school. If anything, these children need recreation, sensitive entertainment, semiorganized activity, and decent care after school. Some ways for a person to discover whether she or he would like to work with children of this age are to volunteer, while still in high school, to coach T-ball or Little League, give swimming lessons, work with the Boy Scouts or Girl Scouts, or join a community center in an arts and crafts program. It is also possible to visit the wards of children's hospitals, do a lot of baby-sitting, or get a counselor job at summer camp.

D. Teenagers

Working with teenagers is exciting and difficult, especially if you are a teenager yourself. Sexuality, music, style, and intellect characterize this time of passage, and you have to be very secure yourself to work with young people passing through the changes that characterize adolescence in our society.

There are many ways to get a feel for what it might be like, from volunteering at literacy programs and drug-dependency peer counseling programs, to participating in student government, working at community centers and at centers for handicapped or disturbed youths, or becoming involved in youth political organizations ranging from Young Democratic and Republican clubs to antinuclear and antiapartheid organizations. Much of the work youths do with other youths is collegial and it is a good way to be exposed to the needs of other young people.

E. Grown-ups

It is somewhat awkward for young people in our society to be in a position to work with and help people from their twen-

· · · · · · · · · · · · ·

ties to their sixties, yet there are ways in which it can happen. For example, reading programs for the blind, food take-in and general companionship programs for housebound and seriously ill people exist. There are also recreational programs for the handicapped, and remedial education programs for them as well. Volunteers are always needed and welcome, and many volunteers end up being hired for longer term, more specialized work. In addition, high school students and graduates are always welcome to help out on newsletters, mailings, leafletting, and designing and distributing posters for service organizations.

F. Seniors

There is a great deal of work high school students and graduates can do to help older people. However, respect is the essence of this work. Older people have seen life, and though some are wiser than others, almost all older people I know have a larger and broader perspective on life than us younger ones. When working with older people one has to be sensitive to the fact that, though older people tend to be physically weaker than younger people, they have lived more and know more. They should be looked on as teachers, and their life experience valued. Also their physical problems must be understood and the pain that goes with aging has to be respected. It is very hard for many old people to internalize the fact that they can no longer do, physically, what they were once capable of, and yet be able to remember the days when they were fully functional. Working with older people requires a desire to learn from their experience as well as patience with the physical and biological needs aging creates.

Life Conditions

Age is not the only consideration when thinking about working with people. Conditions of life vary and it is important to discover the kind of people you feel comfortable working with and helping. There are some people, for example, who are magical with people who have severe handicaps, and others who simply do not feel comfortable working with them. There are some people who can work in cultural settings that are very different than the one they grew up in, and others who only feel at ease with people whose values and style are similar to their own. None of these preferences is "wrong" or "bad." It is just a question of knowing where you can make the greatest contribution and feel enriched by doing it. The following categories of types of people is probably not exhaustive, but it provides a beginning way to get people thinking of who they might like to work with.

A. "Normal"

Who's normal? This category is broad, flexible, and not to be taken too seriously. The reason it's included is to point out that there are some individuals who work best with people who do not have any apparent or pressing problems.

For example, there are wonderful charitable organizations throughout the country, and young people are very often welcomed as volunteers and part-time workers. These organizations range from Oxfam to the March of Dimes. There are people who make their living working with such foundations and charitable organizations. These people serve people in need by raising and distributing funds, but do not come into contact with them directly. They also develop and support cultural and social programs. In addition, it is possible to work as a museum guide, as well as participate in the work of political and environmental organizations.

B. Economically Needy

Working with poor people is complicated because poverty is an economic and not an intellectual or emotional condition. There are brilliant people who are poor, loving people who are poor, compassionate people as well as people with dreams and also people who have given up on life and are violent or self-destructive. Poverty does not negate a person's humanity. But there is a culture of poverty, a culture driven by desperation, characterized by distrust of authority and of outsiders. People are forced into poverty (hardly anyone chooses poverty other than for religious reasons), and it is essential to understand that no matter how much you ease some of the pain of being poor, the ultimate enemy is poverty itself. For that reason, unless poverty itself is eliminated, no matter how much you do, as long as you are not poor yourself, you may be looked upon with suspicion by the poor. That doesn't mean that you shouldn't work with them; it's just a reminder that so long as people are still poor, even if they have a little help, they are bound to feel resentful. So long as you can understand this and integrate it into your consciousness as a condition of work with the poor, you can be of use.

To work effectively with poor people you have to understand, on a visceral level, how the people you serve experience the world. You have to learn how to respect the people you work with in the same way you respect your own family and friends. This is not an easy thing for many people of goodwill. It requires sensitivity to the risk of becoming condescending and patronizing toward the people you work with. On the other hand, the rewards of seeing people in pain become stronger and escape the pains of poverty are enormous.

The main characteristics of middle-class people I have known who do continued good work in poor communities are persistence, a combination of gentleness and toughness, an ability to be tough in dealing with public bureaucracies that serve poor people, and a solid dose of altruism. They do not want to make poor people over in their own images and want to learn as much as to give.

Settlement houses, soup kitchens, centers that aid the homeless, and local Ys are good places to begin, as are social service agencies. Many churches have programs for the poor and homeless as well, and it is a good idea to go to a church that has a social mission and ask the minister how you can get involved.

However, it is essential to realize that working with the poor is hard, frustrating work unless you are also trying somehow to eliminate poverty.

C. At Risk
(Suicide Prevention, Substance Abuse, Runaways, Rape Victims, Anorexia, Bulimia)

In our society there is no lack of misery, and there are more people in trouble than people available to help them. Working with people at risk is emotionally draining and requires an emotional stability and maturity that is difficult to achieve. However, many young people have had friends at risk and have had experience with helping them. They may also have been at risk themselves and managed to come through their own troubles. A number of people with these experiences, or who have heard about the sufferings of people at risk, want to devote themselves to helping people in serious trouble. If a young person has a desire to be of use to others and might like to have a career helping others, a year after high school working in some organization that is devoted to the support and assistance of people at risk is a sensible way to test her or his convictions. Most of this work is voluntary and there is nothing wrong with working for a year at McDonald's during the day and at a suicide prevention center or phone line at night.

There are many organizations that deal with runaways, and there are runaway houses that often need volunteers. However, working with people at risk requires skill and experience as well as compassion, and it is crucial to find a place where you will get good training if you care to do such sensitive work.

D. Mentally Ill

Working with people who are mentally disturbed can often be a challenge to one's own sanity. It is very important to be sure that young people who have a feel for working with the mentally ill are supervised. However, simply being a consistent and caring companion of someone who does not have a grip on his or her own life is a very rewarding experience and is useful work. There are schools and caring institutions that need help all of the time because of the emotional drain on staff and volunteers. However, it is essential to choose a place to work or

. . . .

volunteer very carefully, because there are cruel, primitive, understaffed, and indifferent institutions that provide custody but not care for the mentally ill. There is so much work to be done in this field, so many different levels of involvement, and so much need that anyone who has a feel for helping the confused and out-of-touch people we designate as mentally ill should be encouraged.

E. Physically Ill

Working with home- or hospital-bound people is a good way to test out whether careers such as nursing, medicine, physical therapy, counseling, or psychology are ones that would make for a satisfying life. Hospitals and outpatient clinics are places to explore. One way to make contact is to speak with the head of the volunteer service of your local hospital. The people who run volunteer services at hospitals and clinics are usually very generous with their time, and welcome help.

F. Handicapped

Some people are naturally drawn to helping others who, through birth or accident, are at a disadvantage in dealing with the everyday demands of ordinary life. There are many different forms of handicap, and it is important to understand these differences when you consider whether you want to work with the handicapped.

Physical handicaps can be caused at birth and can result from accidents at any age. It is important to distinguish physical problems from mental or emotional problems. People such as David Hawkins, the physicist, and Josephine Miles, the poet, suffer from crippling diseases that make it necessary for them to have help with the everyday details of care for their bodies. Yet their minds are as large as the universe.

It's very easy to fall into the fallacy of assuming that because a body is crippled a mind is limited. It is important to know the difference between physical and mental disability and to realize that people with physical disabilities often have enor-

1 5 7

mous intellectual needs because they live in their minds more than people who are mobile and physically independent.

Perceptual handicaps such as deafness and blindness also have nothing whatever to do with intelligence and creativity. Perceptual handicaps lead to alternate forms of constructing an image of the world and communicating with others. The blind tend to have highly developed senses of touch and hearing, and the deaf have managed to create a sophisticated manual language that can express everything oral language can convey. If you wish to work with perceptually handicapped people it is essential that you learn about the way they perceive the world and, for example, know initially at least a bit of sign language or Braille. By respecting the world perceptually handicapped people live in and learning their modes of communication it becomes possible to learn from them as well as assist them.

Mentally handicapped people have a hard time with concepts and ideas we take for granted. Ron Jones, who is the recreational director of the Workshop Center for the Handicapped in San Francisco, and a magician when it comes to working with the mentally handicapped, tells a story that illustrates this. One of the clients of the center, Eddie, was given the job of guarding a door at the gym. A staff member tried to come in through the door and was forcibly prevented from entering. The staff member asked Eddie to apologize for hitting him and Eddie refused. At a staff meeting it was decided that Eddie could not come back to the center because he wouldn't apologize. Eddie was distraught and went to Ron to ask for help. Ron told him that all he had to do was apologize, and Eddie looked at Ron and said, "What is apologize?" Eddie didn't understand the concept and Ron solved the problem by telling Eddie to give the staff member a Coke. The Coke was a gift, an acceptable apology that the staff member could accept and Eddie could understand.

Working with severely retarded people requires respect, ingenuity, and an understanding that the people you work with are struggling to understand what is ordinary to you. Time, space, memory, and recognition can all be problems in the world of the retarded. However, as long as they are not abused, most retarded people have a kind and gentle approach to life we can all learn from. Patience, compassion, and the attempt to reconstruct the world according to the people you work with can lead to effective work and to lasting friendships with retarded people.

G. Gifted

People with special gifts and talents can be nurtured, and it is wonderful for young people to share their talents with people younger than they are. The talented and gifted child needs nurturance as well as the hurting child does. In addition, there is a considerable amount of undiscovered talent in the world, and providing an opportunity for youngsters to explore areas they might be interested in is very valuable. If a high school student has a talent he or she can find as much reward in teaching it as in using it.

A few years ago I taught at an elementary school where our music department was the high school band. I've known young artists who love to teach younger ones, and in the world of computers, the sharing of knowledge is very common.

It's also true that, in the area of the arts and computers, age is less important than skill and knowledge. Young artists and computer buffs sometimes make very good teachers of older people.

One way for people just out of high school to test their desire to teach or tutor is to set themselves up in a small tutoring business that could range anywhere from teaching basketball and baseball to teaching reading or guitar or computer programming. Take something you know and turn it into something to share.

Areas of Work

So far there has been an analysis of the age and type of people one might work with. Another variable is the kind of work one might like to do. There are many different ways to be useful to others and take pleasure in work and it makes sense to think about them and even to take a year or two and experiment with different ways of working with people. The more experience you have and the wider the variety of skills you develop the more you might be able to define work that is uniquely yours. Here are some different ways of working with people:

A. Social Welfare

Broadly interpreted, social welfare services range from helping poor people acquire food, medical care, and housing to working in settlement houses or other community projects that deliver services needed by the poor. It can also consist of volunteering with the Red Cross in disaster aid or working with Traveler's Aid. There are both public and private social welfare organizations and many opportunities to volunteer and even get entry-level jobs without having attended college. Anyone interested in finding out whether they would like to provide social services to others can contact public and private welfare agencies, the Red Cross, the United Way, and other local agencies that use volunteer services. Young people are usually welcomed in such organizations and can learn a great deal from people who have devoted their lives to serving others. In addition, serving others is a great source of personal growth. The barriers that exist between people of different ages in our culture can sometimes be overcome by doing social service. There is so much to be learned outside of school and too few opportunities for young people to learn from their elders. A year working for people who have a lot to teach you is a privilege.

Some Examples of Using the WORK WITH PEOPLE Profile Form

Here are some instances of how the WORK WITH PEOPLE profile form has been used. The partial stories they suggest may help you see how varied careers working with people can be.

Fred

Fred, the son of a friend of our family, spent several years taking care of one of his grandmothers. He decided he wanted to try to work with seniors but he didn't want to do home care or recreation. He wanted to help older people with their rights and medical care because he felt some people had taken advantage of his grandmother and as a consequence she spent the last years of her life in a home with terrible care. As we talked, he drew up the following profile of his preferences:

WORK WITH PEOPLE

Ages of People to Work With	Life Conditions of the People to Work With	Areas of Work	Ways You Can Become Involved
A. Infants	A. ''Normal''	A. Social welfare	A. Volunteer work
		B. Education	
B. Early childhood (2 to 5)	B. Economically needy	C. Politics	B. Summer work
		D. Legal issues	
	C. At risk	E. Recreation	C. Apprenticeships
C. Young children (6 to 12)		F. Study of people	
	D. Mentally ill	G. Travel	D. Entry-level work
D. Teenagers		H. Caring for others	
	E. Physically ill	I. Medicine	E. Semiskilled and skilled work
E. Grown-ups		J. Nutrition and food preparation	
	F. Handicapped		F. Independent study
F. Seniors		K. Transportation	
	G. Gifted	L. Public safety	
		M. Environment	
		N. Ergonomics	
		O. Communications and media	
		P. Organizing	
		Q. Arts	
		R. Sciences	

Fred's Profile

He mentioned that he had never thought about working with handicapped people before but the idea intrigued him. I suggested that, given the profile he developed, he go to the Recreation Center for the Handicapped in San Francisco and the Center for Independent Living in Berkeley and see if they could suggest ways for him to work with handicapped seniors as an advocate of their rights. At present he is exploring spending the summer between his junior and senior years of high school volunteering for the local Welfare Rights Organization with a specific emphasis on helping to obtain benefits for handicapped senior citizens.

Rosalie

Rosalie has several friends who suffer from anorexia and bulimia, and she has been trying for several years to help them. She has no desire to be a therapist but would like to be of use to young women who are suffering from eating disorders. Her concern is that many of them are not acknowledged as having disorders and hide what they are doing. She is concerned about their social welfare, their right to get therapy as well as other kinds of support when they do get help and try to overcome their disturbance. Her profile looks like this:

WORK WITH PEOPLE

Ages of People to Work With	Life Conditions of the People to Work With	Areas of Work	Ways You Can Become Involved
A. Infants	A. "Normal"	A. Social welfare	A. Volunteer work
		B. Education	
B. Early childhood (2 to 5)	B. Economically needy	C. Politics	B. Summer work
		D. Legal issues	
	C. At risk	E. Recreation	C. Apprenticeships
C. Young children (6 to 12)		F. Study of people	
	D. Mentally ill	G. Travel	D. Entry-level work
		H. Caring for others	
D. Teenagers	E. Physically ill	I. Medicine	E. Semiskilled and skilled work
		J. Nutrition and food preparation	
E. Grown-ups	F. Handicapped	K. Transportation	F. Independent study
		L. Public safety	
F. Seniors	G. Gifted	M. Environment	
		N. Ergonomics	
		O. Communications and media	
		P. Organizing	
		Q. Arts	
		R. Sciences	

Rosalie's Profile

Rosalie has discovered that there is an anorexia hot line where young women can call and get advice and hopes to volunteer to work there this summer and investigate the possibilities of a career in social welfare. She also feels a need to know more about the specific medical and psychological nature of bulimia and anorexia, and is trying to find out if there are any classes that could help her.

Later, in the Appendix, I'll share a number of specific suggestions on how to go about finding out what resources are available to you as you seek more information about a specific career. The profiles in the book are only a first step toward defining meaningful work.

Returning to Ralph's profile, let's look at the next area of work it suggests.

B. Education

There are a number of ways to do educational work with children without having a B.A. or teaching credential. There are child-care centers, peer tutoring programs, teaching assistantships (especially at private schools), apprenticeships at schools and care homes, camp jobs, and residential-treatment-center house counselor positions. There are also paid teacher-aide and playground jobs in most school districts. One can also work with old people, tutor nonreaders, read stories in libraries, become involved in reading programs for the blind, and teach anything from chess to rock guitar.

Private schools are good places to look because they do not require that all people with teaching responsibilities have credentials.

It's amazing how much teaching can be done by young people. About ten years ago, when I was principal of an alternative high school in the Berkeley Unified School District, a number of my students came to me with the idea of setting up a small primary school for children who were having difficulties. The students wanted to do everything from teach reading to develop science, math, theater, nutrition, and recreation programs for twenty five-, six-, and seven-year-olds. They agreed to let me and a few other teachers from the school district supervise them and for a year ran a wonderful minischool. Somehow their students, who couldn't relate to regular classroom situations, had no problem dealing with the high school students in an informal educational situation that was more like family than "school." They also made considerable progress academically and inspired their high-school-age teachers to learn as much as possible about teaching techniques.

After that year, most of the high school students graduated and the school district decided to retrench on experimentation, so the minischool never made it to a second year. However, of the six young teachers at the school, two eventually became schoolteachers. The others are performing artists who give individual lessons or teach small classes. They all feel that the experience of running a school, which took up more than half of their high school program, gave them a sense of being useful and in control and a sense that they could do real, meaningful work even though they were young.

Education takes place in many different places and it's useful to make a survey of what is available in your community. In any field, in fact, it is important to reach out and find out what is happening in the community. It is important for young people to learn how to discover work and to interview prospective employers about their expectations and take advantage of the advice they might offer. It's interesting how many adults are willing to share knowledge and advice with young people, but don't, simply because they're not usually asked.

Two Sample Education Profiles

Studying the following two profiles may help those interested in working in education by suggesting some unusual but related job leads; at the least, it can help them brainstorm before tackling their own profiles.

Sample Profile #1 implies that the person who filled it out might like to work with hospital-and home-bound children with

WORK WITH PEOPLE

Ages of People to Work With	Life Conditions of the People to Work With	Areas of Work	Ways You Can Become Involved
A. Infants	A. ``Normal''	A. Social welfare	A. Volunteer work
		B. Education	
B. Early childhood (2 to 5)	B. Economically needy	C. Politics	B. Summer work
		D. Legal issues	
	C. At risk	E. Recreation	C. Apprenticeships
C. Young children (6 to 12)		F. Study of people	
	D. Mentally ill	G. Travel	D. Entry-level work
		H. Caring for others	
D. Teenagers	E. Physically ill	I. Medicine	E. Semiskilled and skilled work
		J. Nutrition and	
E. Grown-ups	F. Handicapped	food preparation	F. Independent study
		K. Transportation	
F. Seniors	G. Gifted	L. Public safety	
		M. Environment	
		N. Ergonomics	
		O. Communications and media	
		P. Organizing	
		Q. Arts	
		R. Sciences	

Sample Profile # 1

serious illnesses. Once a focus is that specific a next step is to figure out where to go for advice about work. For example, this profile suggests that one make inquiries at children's hospitals, the American Cancer Society, the Muscular Dystrophy Association, the March of Dimes, and local medical groups.

Sample Profile #2 (see page 166) shows a desire to work with six- to twelve-year-old gifted children and implies employing some special area of interest of one's own. A tutoring program in a community center, providing lessons in everything from math to music and art to poetry, could be an option. My son, who just graduated from high school, gave guitar lessons to children six to eight years old at our local Art Center this summer, and one of our neighbor's children is working with a local children's theater. In addition, a small group of high school computer buffs we know has set up computer lessons for young children. Tutoring can be done in the context of a formal

. . . .

WORK WITH PEOPLE

Ages of People to Work With	Life Conditions of the People to Work With	Areas of Work	Ways You Can Become Involved
A. Infants	A. "Normal"	A. Social welfare	A. Volunteer work
		B. Education	
B. Early childhood (2 to 5)	B. Economically needy	C. Politics	B. Summer work
		D. Legal issues	
	C. At risk	E. Recreation	C. Apprenticeships
C. Young children (6 to 12)		F. Study of people	
	D. Mentally ill	G. Travel	D. Entry-level work
		H. Caring for others	
D. Teenagers	E. Physically ill	I. Medicine	E. Semiskilled and skilled work
		J. Nutrition and food preparation	
E. Grown-ups	F. Handicapped	K. Transportation	F. Independent study
		L. Public safety	
F. Seniors	G. Gifted	M. Environment	
		N. Ergonomics	
		O. Communications and media	
		P. Organizing	
		Q. Arts	
		R. Sciences	

Sample Profile #2

program or at home. An ad in the local newspaper will often bring in enough students to begin one's own program.

C. Politics

Political parties are always looking for volunteers, and volunteer work in politics can often lead to part-time jobs and even full-time work in legislatures or in politics on a local level. Early involvement in politics is also one way to get an intimate look at the best and worst of adults outside of one's family and school. In addition, high school graduates, who have lived for years among people who are very close to them in age and ideas, have opportunities, during political campaigns, to meet older people who do a wide variety of things.

Political work might involve everything from polling to running a telephone tree to postering and leafletting. It can consist of setting up grandstands and sound systems for rallies or running a sound truck. It can also involve addressing envelopes, taking notes at meetings, recruiting new members, registering voters, and even giving speeches about your candidate.

The easiest time to get involved in politics is during an election campaign, when there is always a need for people. The best time, however, is probably when there is no pending election. Things are much quieter then and it is possible to get to know professional campaign workers more intimately because they have more time to train young people and show them how to get around in politics.

In terms of Ralph's profile, of course, there is little to do in politics with infants, other than perhaps helping candidates kiss babies or taking pictures of them doing it. However, political education, voter registration, and work with groups such as Common Cause or the League of Women Voters can be rewarding and lead to contacts that might point one toward a vocation.

D. Legal Issues

The image of the lawyer who uses litigation for his or her own personal gain is a limited way to look at the profession. There are environmental lawyers, lawyers who work with nonprofit corporations, others who do advocacy law for issues ranging from homelessness to racial prejudice. There are public prosecutors and public defenders as well as corporate and insurance lawyers. And, at the high school level, a number of youngsters are what could be called schoolhouse lawyers. They defend their rights and the rights of other students and are often considered defiant and difficult because of it. They are lawyers and don't know it. It might be useful for some youngsters to visit lawyers, both public and private, in their community and see whether paid or voluntary work is available that would provide them with a working knowledge of what is involved with being a lawyer. Certainly Nader's Raiders, the Sierra Club, the Environmental Policy Institute, and other advocacy groups need volunteers or gofers. And the same might be true for some corporate law firms.

A DESCRIPTION AND ANALYSIS OF THE PROFILES

. . . .

An Exercise

To get you thinking about ways to become involved in your chosen area of interest, here is an exercise you can try a few times throughout the rest of this section. Even if you aren't directly interested in the area under discussion, doing the exercise may still yield a couple of good ideas—and it's a good way to stretch your imagination before doing your own profile.

Take this blank profile form (it's best to use a photocopy) and draw a line from "Legal issues" (in the third column) to any entry in the second column, and from there to any entry in the first column. Then list several ways in which a high school student or recent graduate can get involved in the work the profile represents.

WORK WITH PEOPLE

Ages of People to Work With	Life Conditions of the People to Work With	Areas of Work	Ways You Can Become Involved
A. Infants	A. "Normal"	A. Social welfare B. Education	A. Volunteer work
B. Early childhood (2 to 5)	B. Economically needy	C. Politics D. Legal issues	B. Summer work
C. Young children (6 to 12)	C. At risk D. Mentally ill	E. Recreation F. Study of people G. Travel	C. Apprenticeships D. Entry-level work
D. Teenagers	E. Physically ill	H. Caring for others I. Medicine J. Nutrition and	E. Semiskilled and skilled work
E. Grown-ups	F. Handicapped	food preparation K. Transportation	F. Independent study
F. Seniors	G. Gifted	L. Public safety M. Environment N. Ergonomics O. Communications and media P. Organizing Q. Arts R. Sciences	

Blank Profile Form

.

1 6 8

. . . .

Here's one example of a completed profile:

WORK WITH PEOPLE

Ages of People to Work With	Life Conditions of the People to Work With	Areas of Work	Ways You Can Become Involved
A. Infants	A. "Normal"	A. Social welfare B. Education	A. Volunteer work
B. Early childhood (2 to 5)	B. Economically needy	C. Politics D. Legal issues	B. Summer work
C. Young children (6 to 12)	C. At risk D. Mentally ill	E. Recreation F. Study of people G. Travel	C. Apprenticeships D. Entry-level work
D. Teenagers	E. Physically ill	H. Caring for others I. Medicine J. Nutrition and	E. Semiskilled and skilled work
E. Grown-ups	F. Handicapped	food preparation K. Transportation	F. Independent study
F. Seniors	G. Gifted	L. Public safety M. Environment N. Ergonomics O. Communications and media P. Organizing Q. Arts R. Sciences	

Sample Profile

The profile is of someone who might like to work with poor older people and help them with their legal rights. Several possibilities come to mind: volunteer work at local legal services organizations; legal secretary training and work in firms that do advocacy for the poor; involvement with seniors' organizations, such as the Gray Panthers, in terms of the legal issues they face. In each of these cases, it makes sense to visit organizations and talk to people about what you might be able to do, and to follow the trail of suggestions until something emerges. For example, someone might start with legal services for the homeless and end up with a local public-advocacy housing group or a corporate law firm that takes on young people as apprentices as part of its public service contribution.

Drawing up random profiles as an exercise has the value of getting you used to imagining ways of defining forms of work and thinking of ways to gather resources. It might be called a "Chinese menu" approach to developing vocational imagination: Choose one thing from each column and then imagine the jobs that are defined by that profile and the places where one can find out about them.

E. Recreation

Work in recreation can be found anywhere from the playground to the pool hall and the hospital to the retirement home. Sometimes young people don't realize that they have usable talents. For people who love to use their bodies, or play games, there is a world of potential work that is not usually validated in school. There are fields ranging from sports medicine to physical rehabilitation, coaching, and the design and manufacture of sports equipment, as well as the invention of games, that are worth examining if you have an affinity for them. The most important thing is to have a wide vision of what you might do and be bold in approaching people who are already involved in things you find intriguing. Sometimes something as informal as hanging out at a place and talking to people who work there can lead to work and to contacts.

F. Study of People

Some people enjoy studying the personal and social aspects of life and gathering information. The work they can do is both interesting and useful. There are opportunities for young people to explore fields such as ethnography, anthropology, and survey research without having been to college. Here are some possibilities:

- working or volunteering on an archaeological dig
- doing fieldwork for a marketing research firm
- doing polling on political and social issues
- working with the U.S. Census Bureau
- working for telephone polling organizations

Some time spent doing work like this can lead to a career or at least to some insight into society that might not be obtained at fast-food chains.

G. Travel

Travel can be healing as well as broadening. It used to be traditional, for young people who could afford it, to take a "grand tour" before settling down to college, work, or marriage. Living in a culture that is different, meeting people who are not from one's own community or country, can be a challenge to define yourself as well as a source of pleasure. There are jobs as travel companions, au pairs, and baby-sitters, as well as other jobs teaching English or house-sitting that can support a year or two of travel. There is also seasonal work in Europe, such as picking grapes or tulip bulbs, and in Alaska during the summer in the fishing industry.

There are also many Peace Corps–like experiences that are sponsored by churches and other service organizations that can lead to work throughout the world. In the Appendix there is a list of organizations that can be contacted in order to set up exchanges or international work experiences.

In my experience, traveling time is never wasted time. On the contrary, it creates a sense of independence and largeness that can help you sort out vocational and personal choices. One way to enrich travel is to focus on a particular area of work in the places you visit and, for example, go to schools, or rehabilitation centers, or visit theater and arts workshops or computer centers. These are good places to meet people and also provide a perspective on the way similar activities are usually done in the United States.

H. Caring for Others

There are many people who need home care, meals brought in, shopping done for them. There are also people in nursing homes or retirement homes who long for companionship on a regular basis. Some people simply need someone to read to them or visit with them and chat casually. There are many volunteer organizations that will connect young people with people in need of care and companionship, and learning to care for someone can lead to a career in caring professions such as geriatrics, nursing, paramedical work, medicine, and counseling.

I. Medicine

There is a lot of volunteer work at hospitals and there are also CPR and other training classes that allow young people to become paramedics or work at clinics and hospitals. Becoming a doctor is a long, hard haul, and a year's work in the field before deciding whether to pursue a medical career is probably a wise thing to do. Even if ultimately you decide to pursue some other vocation, that year can provide invaluable experience and maturity through contact with both patients and the many different kinds of people whose work consists of healing.

Some ways to find out about what might be possible are to contact the local branch of the American Medical Association, local nurses' organizations, and the hospital workers' unions. Ambulance and emergency care companies also can be contacted. Local colleges and junior colleges that give paramedic classes are also good sources of information. You could sign on with an emergency medical mission to a disaster area, work with an international health organization giving vaccinations, or join the military medical corps.

When searching for information, don't just talk to people on the phone. Audit classes, make appointments to talk with people in person, and visit medical centers and hospitals. It never hurts to take the initiative and show your interest.

J. Nutrition and Food Preparation

People have to eat, and they spend a lot of money and ingenuity figuring out ways to make that regular experience interesting. The restaurant, catering, and food-preparation industry provides opportunities for young people to get a feel for food preparation. Unfortunately, the most common entry job is washing dishes, but that's not to be scorned. Someone who is serious about food will usually move on to other work in or out of the kitchen.

Nutrition is another field that can be pursued. There are health inspectors, nutritionists who prepare balanced and special menus for people who have special nutritional needs or who test the nutritional values of foods that are marketed. There are meals-on-wheels programs for the elderly and home-bound, and voluntary programs that feed the poor. The federal and state governments have bureaus of standards, and cities have health and nutrition departments. There are many ways to volunteer or to find entry-level jobs in the field of nutrition without a college degree, and, once again, it doesn't hurt to spend a year exploring whether you would like to spend a life doing something.

K. Transportation

Some people like to drive. A simple way to satisfy this need is to drive cars across the country for people who are moving. It's also possible to drive buses, cabs, trains, boats, planes. It's possible to become a bike messenger or a bike racer. Unfortunately, many jobs in transportation are limited to people over twenty-one because of insurance laws. This varies from state to state, and it's important to explore local laws.

L. Public Safety

From traffic control to fire control, there are many useful things to do in the field. During the summer, for example, many states hire temporary firefighters to deal with the inevitable forest fires. There is always a need for people to monitor parking meters or help with highway construction or work on telephone and electrical lines. With an open attitude toward work, many unexpected jobs can open up. For example, I have some friends who work for Pacific Gas and Electric who have college degrees but find a decent and challenging life clearing downed electrical lines after storms and putting in new ones. Others work part-time at the local fire and police departments.

M. Environment

There is too much to clean up in our society. There are many environmental groups a young person can either volunteer or work for, and the work can range from stuffing envelopes to cleaning up birds after an oil spill, climbing a chimney in protest of industrial pollution, or trying to prevent the killing of baby seals. There also are many scientific, managerial, and political careers that can emerge from environmental work. Work on environmental management ranges from apprenticeships in government (for instance, on environmental subcommittees of state senates and assemblies) to doing research and writing for advocacy groups. They can encompass public relations, technical writing, or survey research, as well as participation in wildlife management experiments. The best thing to do is look up environmental groups in the Yellow Pages of your phone book (there is a listing for them) and visit them.

N. Ergonomics

Ergonomics is the study and development of working environments that are planned around the needs of people. It deals with things such as designing the right-sized chairs for five-year-olds and the right placement of computer screens to protect the eyes of the people who work with them. Making playground equipment, designing and building school furniture, and doing gracious landscaping are all ways to begin to explore human-scale design—that is, ergonomics. There are many companies that deal with the redesign of environments, and once one gets into a company all kinds of opportunities can open up, ranging from the development of one's own small business to the desire to get a degree in architecture or environmental design.

To get information, begin by calling the department of architecture or the school of environmental design at a local university and asking for the names of local firms and people who do ergonomic or human-scale design.

O. Communications and Media

Public and private newspapers and radio and TV stations sometimes take on young apprentices. There are also college radio stations, pirate radio stations, underground papers, small presses, print shops, and film and video studios that function on modest levels. If you think you would like a career in the media, you need time to learn the craft, understand the standards demanded by it, and practice skills. It is better to jump into the business than to wait until college is over if you have no other reason to go to college.

There are private broadcasting and media schools that give classes and do not require college or any prior experience. However, one has to be careful about the reliability of such schools. It's worth looking into them carefully as well as going straight to local newspapers and broadcasting stations and inquiring about volunteer or entry-level work or apprenticeships.

Public radio and television have apprenticeship programs, and Pacifica radio stations depend on volunteer work. In fact, a number of the most successful reporters on National Public Radio began as volunteers at Pacifica.

P. Organizing

Many problems, such as homelessness, poverty, AIDS, the rights of minorities, and the peace movement, need people's time and energy. Giving a year or two of one's life to working on social problems and helping people organize advocacy groups to solve them is invaluable experience. Many community and nationwide organizations try to deal with such social problems and usually need all the help they can get. Working in these organizations can help develop skills in conflict resolution and negotiation. They also give good training in systems management, budgeting and fund-raising, and organizational structure. Many business and administrative skills are very useful in working with community organizations, and a young person who wants to develop and practice these skills will find herself welcome in many community service organizations.

Q. Arts

One can work with people through performance. On a simple level one may entertain at birthday parties, run summer art programs, give music or art lessons, put on or act in community plays, publish a local magazine. If you're in a band, it's possible to play at parties and weddings as well as clubs. There is very valuable experience to be obtained by doing a lot of little things and not expecting to be a superstar—right off the bat, at any rate. Teaching and performing for community benefits are also effective ways to make contacts that can help in pursuing a career in the arts.

R. Sciences

A number of scientific careers involve working with people. For example, many of the social, health, and environmental sciences concentrate on the ways in which scientific knowledge can be used to understand people and the world and to discover ways to nurture the earth. Urgent issues such as acid rain, the greenhouse effect, chemical pollution, water management, and the AIDS epidemic must be dealt with using scientific information and techniques. Researchers need young people who are willing to devote their lives to doing research and participating in action projects relating to these major crises. Many organizations are devoted to supporting this research and action, and among the resources listed in the Appendix are avenues you can follow for information about these careers.

Ways You Can Become Involved

There are many ways to begin to explore vocation after high school. This is quite different than just getting a job. Too often, parents are so disappointed when their children decide

• • • • • • • • • • • • •

not to attend college that they take out their frustration by insisting that their children get a job, any job. But it makes more sense to continue to support children and help them explore their vocational preferences instead of punishing them for not knowing what they want to do with their lives.

A. Volunteer Work

In doing research on this book I've discovered that an excellent route to many different kinds of work comes through volunteering. Most of the keepers and handlers at the San Francisco Zoo began as volunteers, for example, and a number of people who are currently on public radio took the volunteer route as well. In the theater, at charitable organizations, in athletics, and at social services agencies a good number of people find work through the route of volunteering first.

A good volunteer is someone who shows up on time, does menial work agreeably, and asks the right questions. There is always a place for a good worker in a serious public service operation or an artistic community. Start small, spend time, work hard, and there is a good chance that a job will emerge within a year if a volunteer does good work and becomes indispensable.

If you are poor you don't have the option to volunteer, but even then, half-time work for money and half-time volunteering may be possible.

B. Summer Work

Some temporary summer jobs are very challenging and can lead to other possibilities. For example, I have known young people whose lives have been influenced by fighting forest fires during the summer, or working in the canneries in Alaska, or becoming guides in national forests or museums. Others have worked as theater ushers, apprentices in art galleries, and gofers (going for lunch, for coffee, and for anything else they are asked to go for) in record or movie studios or publishing houses. You can find summer work if you look around, present yourself well, show interest in the work and respect for the people you might work for.

C. Apprenticeships

Getting an apprenticeship is usually a matter of having contacts, charm, or tact, though sometimes having skills helps. There is no harm trying to get an apprenticeship in even the most unlikely places. It is often a matter of how you present yourself. I've known young people who've dropped out of high school but were able to convince university scientists to take them on as apprentices and give them work as lab assistants, young musicians who got work as roadies while learning the music business, and young writers who managed to become apprenticed as readers or even stock clerks at major publishing houses. I remember having an apprentice job organizing filing cards for a new edition of *Roget's Thesaurus* for Crowell publishers. It was boring and didn't pay much, but I learned a great deal about the publishing industry just being there.

D. Entry-Level Work

Much can be learned from a year or two as a stock clerk in a record company or quality record store, in the shipping department of a computer manufacturer, as a laborer on a construction job, or as a car mechanic or door-to-door salesperson. Getting into the world of work on a beginning level and exploring who one is by how one does on the job is often more valuable than spending more time in school or trying to make lots of money fast. Respect for decent work comes from experiences with different types of work, and love for work comes from knowing yourself through what you like to do. As long as you keep your eyes open when you're working, and watch how other people work, and learn the structure of the business, even the simplest entry-level job can become a vehicle for valuable learning.

·

1 7 8

E. Semiskilled and Skilled Work

Many young people develop skills through their hobbies or private obsessions. I've known young people who've learned to do everything from bicycle and auto repair to comic book coloring and computer programming outside of school. And many of these young people have become professionals at those crafts and used them as ways to earn money while developing either those or other skills for their futures. One young man I know is a professional comic book colorist at the age of nineteen (working for major comic book companies), and he has raised enough money to stake himself to several years at art college, where he plans to go next fall. Another used his skill repairing bicycles and motorcycles to support himself while he went to school to get a contractor's license. Many of the model builders in the film industry began as home modelists, and youngsters I know who used to love to make toys and dolls now make a sustaining living creating and selling crafts to fairs.

It seems to me it's essential that we learn how to validate the skills young people do have and help them use those skills and affinities as bases upon which they can build their futures.

F. Independent Study

Many high schools have independent study programs that allow self-motivated students to study subjects not offered at their schools, and to choose teachers who are not necessarily employed by public school systems. These programs can allow people to take classes ranging from city planning to aerobics and from topology to making tofu. They also allow students to get credit for off-campus learning.

Usually what is required is to get a teacher or counselor at the high school to agree to be the supervisor and liaison. Independent study programs can range from taking junior college or correspondence classes (from the University of Nebraska or the University of California, for example) to working as an apprentice at an electronics firm, learning to be a sous-chef at a restaurant, or working at an automobile body shop. Medical centers, radio and TV stations, local newspapers, museums, law firms, and retail businesses also often offer study possibilities. Independent study can be tailored to a student and, depending on the attitude of your high school administration, can provide, during the junior and senior years of high school, at least half the credit you need to graduate. In the states where it is allowed, it can be a wonderful resource for the exploration of possible futures.

I've worked with students on independent study for several years and found it possible to plan my work with them in a way that was useful to me and at the same time a decent learning experience for the students. I've taught word processing, helped students learn how to create a small magazine, and taught writing and algebra. My daughter Tonia graduated from high school a year early by taking independent study correspondence classes from the University of Nebraska and spent what would have been her senior year in high school going to art school.

A SAMPLE PROFILE

Here is a sample profile that was developed with Julia, a high school junior. Julia had the "I don't know what I want to do and don't know what there is to do" syndrome, but she did know that she wanted to do something people-oriented. We went through the profile form, and communicating with everybody intrigued her. She said she would love to have some kind of apprenticeship at a newspaper or radio or TV station if possible, but that she'd settle for a newsletter for some small group if that would help her learn how to write and publish. Given that she was a junior in high school and intended to get her diploma the next year, it made sense for her to try for a summer apprenticeship, and in the Bay Area where she lives, Pacifica Radio and National Public Radio do take on summer apprentices and interns. She was able to volunteer in the engineering room at Pacifica, and helped prepare the evening news on occasion.

. . . .

Not every community has these resources, but community and church groups everywhere need help with newsletters, and print shops tend to welcome young apprentices. Local newspapers also often encourage high school students to write columns about student events, gossip, and social notes.

WORK WITH PEOPLE

Ages of People to Work With	Life Conditions of the People to Work With	Areas of Work	Ways You Can Become Involved
A. Infants	A. "Normal"	A. Social welfare	A. Volunteer work
		B. Education	
B. Early childhood (2 to 5)	B. Economically needy	C. Politics	B. Summer work
		D. Legal issues	
C. Young children (6 to 12)	C. At risk	E. Recreation	C. Apprenticeships
		F. Study of people	
	D. Mentally ill	G. Travel	D. Entry-level work
		H. Caring for others	
D. Teenagers	E. Physically ill	I. Medicine	E. Semiskilled and skilled work
		J. Nutrition and	
E. Grown-ups	F. Handicapped	food preparation	F. Independent study
		K. Transportation	
F. Seniors	G. Gifted	L. Public safety	
		M. Environment	
		N. Ergonomics	
		O. Communications and media	
		P. Organizing	
		Q. Arts	
		R. Sciences	

Julia's Profile

.

Profile Form 2:
WORK
IN MEDIA
AND
THE ARTS

WORK IN MEDIA AND THE ARTS

Areas of Work	Modes	Places of Work	Ways You Can Become Involved
A. Writing	A. Creation	A. Studio	A. Volunteer work
B. TV and radio	B. Performance		
C. Film and video	C. Direction	B. Business	B. Summer work
D. Photography	D. Design		
E. Music	E. Technical crafts	C. College/school	C. Apprenticeships
F. Theater	F. Editorial		
G. Dance	G. Criticism	D. Community center	D. Entry-level work
H. Fiber arts and fashion	H. Production		
I. Painting and printmaking	I. Administration	E. Home	E. Semiskilled and skilled work
J. Sculpture and 3-dimensional art	J. Publicity and sales	F. Organizations	F. Independent study
K. Industrial and commercial design	K. Running a venue	G. TV/radio network or station	
L. Jewelry, glass, and ceramics	L. Manager/agent	H. Theater	
M. Crafts	M. Manufacturing	I. Production center	
		J. Craft fairs	

PROFILE FORM #2

FOR THE past two years, I've watched the development of a local reggae band. The band started out with a self-taught drummer and bass guitar player, an electric keyboard player who had taken four or five years of piano lessons, and a lead guitarist/singer who had taken guitar lessons but was completely self-taught as a vocalist. Two of the musicians were seniors in high school and two had just graduated. They practiced in their families' garages for several months and then began to play at friends' parties.

There were several musicians from a band named Bland Babies at one of these parties, and they asked our local band, which decided to call itself Roof Rock, to give them a phone number because they might have a gig for them. A few days later a young woman, Sage, who was a senior at another high school, called the bassist. It seems she had set herself up as a band manager and agent, and did booking for a number of groups that were just coming out of the garages and beginning to play for money. She said that she could book them to open for Bland Babies at a local cabaret and pay them ten dollars each for the night. They jumped at the opportunity and played their first "professional" performance.

Sage got Roof Rock a number of club bookings, and after a few months they began to be the featured band and had other bands opening for them. They developed a following and saved the money they earned to buy better equipment. One of their friends, who wasn't a musician, volunteered to take care of the equipment, set up the speakers, and do all of the wiring and monitoring of sound. After a few performances he became the band's technician, and a few weeks after that, the band bought a reverb he recommended that produced special electronic effects while the band was performing.

During the course of their first year of professional performance the band added another musician—a trumpet player who was an experienced musician in his forties. He helped with arrangements and tightened up their sound.

The band was very successful and after a while Roof Rock rented facilities and produced its own performances. This meant they had to pay friends to make and distribute posters, set up and decorate the hall, take money at the door, do other publicity, be bouncers, and help with the transportation of equipment.

After another year, the band decided to produce its own tapes and T-shirts, and sell them at performances, since that would double or triple the amount of money they earned. That meant working with silk screen artists, T-shirt wholesalers, studio technicians, and tape reproduction companies as well as the designer, photographer, and printer who did the liner for the tape and the advertising poster to go along with it.

In the two years they were together professionally, the members of the band improved their musical skills and learned how to plan a performance and perform under differing and sometimes difficult conditions. They also learned how to run a small business effectively and deal with club owners, shirt and tape manufacturers, and banks. In addition, many other people, who loved music and weren't musicians, found useful ways to become involved with the band and be part of the music world. In all there were perhaps fifteen young people involved in a direct way with Roof Rock.

After two years the band split up. One of the original band members went to college to study psychology; another went to college to study music and writing. A third member of the band decided to travel for a year, and the fourth joined another band. None of them would have given up that time together to go to college right after high school. They all agree that the experience was "not merely educational, but wonderful."

I began this section on working in the arts and in media with a look at Roof Rock in order to point out the variety of skills and diversity of roles people can play in the media. Working in music does not just mean being a musician, just as being involved in painting and other graphic arts does not necessarily mean being a painter or graphic artist. The same holds true for working in TV or radio, for being in the theater, or for designing clothes, toys, jewelry, or furniture. In all the arts and media occupations there are technical specialists, teachers, managers, administrators, agents and editors, producers, critics, and publicity people as well as functioning artists. And there are people who enjoy these different roles and do their life's work as some part of the community of arts and media workers. A person does not have to be an artist to dream about a life engaged in the arts.

The arts and media profile form reproduced in this section tries to capture some of the complexity of work in the arts and media. It does not restrict itself to dealing with performers or creative artists but tries to encompass most of the modes of work that make the arts accessible to the public and performances possible. When you conceive of the arts and media in this broad a context, it becomes easy to understand that over a million people are employed full-time (and many more part-time) in the arts and media, which, together, form one of the largest segments of our economy.

Before considering the individual components of the profile form, let's look at some specific profiles in order to get a feel for how a young person might get involved in work in this area.

The first profile (see page 186) was filled out by Sage, the manager and booking agent for Roof Rock.

Sage was clear about wanting to be part of the music world, but had no desire to be a musician. She liked to manage, to know the performers, and to have the feeling that she could nurture people to success. One of her preferences was to be an agent for several bands or a broker who made arrangements between venues (places to perform such as clubs and parties) and the musicians themselves. She also liked the idea that she could do that work out of her bedroom, using her own phone, and make contacts by going to shows. She learned from her mother, who was a CPA, that it always helped to have a business card, and so she printed up her own cards even before she made any money as an agent. Finally, she thought she would like to spend some time as an apprentice at a large musicians' agency and expand her knowledge of the field.

As we went through the profile, another route to involvement in the music world occurred to her. She said that one of her dreams was to own a club of her own and discover new talents and introduce them to more established performers. In

WORK IN MEDIA AND THE ARTS

Areas of Work	Modes	Places of Work	Ways You Can Become Involved
A. Writing	A. Creation	A. Studio	A. Volunteer work
B. TV and radio	B. Performance		
C. Film and video	C. Direction	B. Business	B. Summer work
D. Photography	D. Design		
E. Music	E. Technical crafts	C. College/school	C. Apprenticeships
F. Theater	F. Editorial		
G. Dance	G. Criticism	D. Community center	D. Entry-level work
H. Fiber arts and fashion	H. Production		
I. Painting and printmaking	I. Administration	E. Home	E. Semiskilled and skilled work
J. Sculpture and 3-dimensional art	J. Publicity and sales		
K. Industrial and commercial design	K. Running a venue	F. Organizations	F. Independent study
L. Jewelry, glass, and ceramics	L. Manager/agent	G. TV/radio network or station	
M. Crafts	M. Manufacturing	H. Theater	
		I. Production center	
		J. Craft fairs	

Sage's Profile

fact, she said, maybe she should do more than be an agent; she should try to work at a club and see what it took to make a profit and still discover talent.

These days Sage still books bands and has a part-time job at a local cabaret where she helps bands set up, covers the door sometimes, does the publicity, and even, in cases of emergencies, serves pizza and beer. She has also enrolled at the local junior college in two classes that deal with running small businesses. It's possible she might even get her own club one day.

JONATHAN

Jonathan has very different things in mind. He's been playing with computer graphics for about five years and is a film and comic book buff. His dream is to do special effects for film or TV, and he would love to work in a studio or at a broadcasting

. . . .

WORK IN MEDIA AND THE ARTS

Areas of Work	Modes	Places of Work	Ways You Can Become Involved
A. Writing	A. Creation	A. Studio	A. Volunteer work
B. TV and radio	B. Performance		
C. Film and video	C. Direction	B. Business	B. Summer work
D. Photography	D. Design		
E. Music	E. Technical crafts	C. College/school	C. Apprenticeships
F. Theater	F. Editorial		
G. Dance	G. Criticism	D. Community center	D. Entry-level work
H. Fiber arts and fashion	H. Production		
I. Painting and printmaking	I. Administration	E. Home	E. Semiskilled and skilled work
J. Sculpture and 3-dimensional art	J. Publicity and sales	F. Organizations	F. Independent study
K. Industrial and commercial design	K. Running a venue	G. TV/radio network or station	
L. Jewelry, glass, and ceramics	L. Manager/agent	H. Theater	
M. Crafts	M. Manufacturing	I. Production center	
		J. Craft fairs	

Jonathan's Profile

station. He's also willing to volunteer or take an apprenticeship, which he knows will be very hard to get.

He visited all of the film and broadcasting studios he could and found nothing. Then he went to all of the local, small video production companies he could find, and he found one that produced documentaries for public-access TV. They welcomed him because they were always short of staff. After a while they let him play with their editing machine and computer and figure out some special effects for their programming.

Jonathan says that when he finishes the year he may go to engineering school or try to use his experience to get an entry-level job working for a bigger company.

When developing your profile it's important to consider more than one route if at all possible. Take the time to examine all of the things you might like to do with your life, and reflect upon them before deciding which ones to pursue. Often creative syntheses emerge from this reflection. For example, someone who started out wanting to work with animals or be a musician might find a way to put those two interests together and decide on trying to study and reproduce animal sounds and communication.

THE WORK IN MEDIA AND THE ARTS PROFILE

There are four columns on the chart. The one on the farthest right, "Ways You Can Become Involved," is the same as that column on the WORK WITH PEOPLE profile form. You might want to take another look at the description of the entries in that column in the previous chapter.

The column second from the right refers to the places where work in the arts and media might take place. Here is a brief description of the entries in that column.

Places of Work

A. Studio

There are a number of different types of artists' studios, ranging from recording studios to video, film, ceramics, acting, painting, design, woodworking, sculpture, and other studios. The studio is the place where the work is done, not where it is performed, displayed, or sold (though sometimes artists have studio sales, opening their studios to visitors and selling their work without using an intermediary). Some artists never come out of the studio, and there are musicians, too, who do not perform in public but work in recording studios playing on albums or sound tracks for videos and films.

B. Business

Arts and media businesses range all the way from galleries to shops and boutiques, bookstores, and other outlets for the work that artists do. Art businesses also include art supply stores and record and videotape shops.

C. College/School

Art and media colleges, schools, academies, and conservatories are teaching places. They include formal colleges and conservatories such as the Rhode Island School of Design, Pratt Institute, Juilliard, the San Francisco State University Media Arts Center, and the film departments of UCLA and UVSC. These institutions, which are difficult to get into, usually provide four-year B.F.A. (Bachelor of Fine Arts) programs, the content of which is about 75 percent theory and 25 percent practice of one of the arts. There are also many private art schools and musical academies, as well as individual teachers in all the arts and media on all levels of skill. Many practicing artists teach as well as create their own works. In fact, for beginning artists in all fields, teaching is one modest source of income that helps you get by while you're honing your skills and establishing a reputation.

D. Community Center

Community centers often have arts programs, put on community-based shows, or book people to perform in small communities that don't have arts programs of their own. They also provide lessons, peer groups of artists, discussion groups, and exhibit space and studios at modest prices. Working at a community center is a good entry job in the arts community, and the facilities many of the centers provide make it possible for a young person with small resources to have a place to work and perform or exhibit.

E. Home

Working at home is another way to get started in the arts. A garage or a spare room can become a studio—and a classroom as well. It's great fun for a teenager to build her or his own studio, and it's cheaper than renting a space. The disadvantage for a young person of just working at home is that it is lonely and isolated from the world of other young artists who can enrich and criticize one's work. Mixing work at home with taking classes, or participating in programs at a community center, or working at a shop, is perhaps a better option. Of course, if you're in a band or part of a theater troupe, the home studio can become a practice hall for the whole group, and one can perform in any number of other venues.

F. Organizations

Arts and media organizations provide opportunities to work in the fields of arts administration, funding, and program development. They provide experience in writing proposals, setting up fund-raising benefits, and developing conferences and meetings. These organizations are frequently in need of volunteers, and some may take apprentices. Examples of such organizations in the field of writing are the California Poets in the Schools in San Francisco, the Teachers and Writers Collaborative in New York, and COMPAS in St. Paul. The National Council of the Arts in Washington is made up of state councils and is one of the largest arts organizations in the country. On a more episodic level, organizations like Bill Graham Productions in San Francisco put on benefits, and recently there have been ad hoc organizations created to sponsor benefits like Live Aid and Farm Aid. A good way to find out about these organizations is to begin with your state's Council on the Arts or the Yellow Pages or one of the directories of organizations mentioned in the Appendix to this book.

G. TV/Radio Network or Station

TV and radio networks and local stations produce and broadcast programs. If you are persistent and are interested in being on the air or playing some business or technical role in the broadcast industry, you should dog people in the business and develop a repertoire of your own radio and TV shows. All you need is a tape recorder, a mike or two, and an inexpensive sound mixer (about twenty-five dollars at Radio Shack) for radio, and a home video camera and player for TV.

·

H. Theater

Theaters come in all sizes and shapes and present films, plays, concerts, discussions, lectures, and dances. There are many different jobs people working at theaters perform. Some people do the programming and booking; others manage the door or deal with the finances. Some run the technical side of putting on a performance, and others, of course, perform. Each of these different roles can provide creative challenges. Good programming and stable finances, for example, are essential to keeping the arts and media alive and thriving.

I. Production Center

Production centers are different from studios and places for exhibit or performance. A production center is a place where film mastering and reproduction, tape and record duplication and packaging, poster and art duplication, and printing take place. There are foundries where metal sculpture is made; glassblowing factories; lithographic, silk screen, and etching facilities; wood and metal shops for furniture making and model building for special effects, as well as theater facilities for making costumes and building sets and props. These production facilities employ skilled craftspeople who take artistic ideas, plans, and models and produce finished products for display, performance, and sale. Often such centers train their own craftspeople, and a skilled young carpenter, seamstress, or metalworker is usually welcome.

J. Craft Fairs

The craft fair circuit is a source of income for many craftspeople and performers. There are harvest fairs, pumpkin fairs, Christmas fairs, and more. At the fairs craftspeople pay for booths and sell their handmade wares, ranging from food to jewelry, dolls, clothes, toys, glassware, puzzles, cribs, chairs, desks, paintings, and posters. Fairs are also good places to make contacts with other craftspeople and artists, as well as retailers and wholesalers who often stock items they discover at the fairs.

Modes

The second column from the left, entitled "Modes," refers to the different functions people play as a creative work goes from inception to public exposure. Some individuals function in more than one mode; others specialize. For example, there are painters who paint, work at or run galleries, and write art criticism, and there are actors who also direct, write, and produce films. In the music business, some performers are excellent technicians, do their own sound mastering, and have their own record labels and mail-order businesses.

Realize that you can play multiple roles in the arts and media, and that your entry into the field can be through any number of different modes of work that relate to your central affinities.

Here is a brief description of the different modes listed in the profile.

A. Creation

Creation is, of course, central to the arts and media. It is the central driving force in the arts, the desire to create a unique work that other individuals will find moving or entertaining. Without a painter, composer, writer, filmmaker, or designer there is no product or performance. Creative artists, however, don't all perform and often don't produce the final product of their conception. Filmmaking, for example, requires many people with multiple skills. Someone may conceive of a film idea, sketch it out, and even create a script, but during the production of the film the ideas and original work will be filtered through the input of actors, directors, cinematographers, designers, and production and marketing people.

B. Performance

Many creative works depend essentially on live or taped performances. The performing artist has special skills that distinguish her or him from the creator of a work of art. Performers must be able to work before an audience and present themselves in ways that audiences can respond to. Though they might be personally shy, they have to be able to interpret the work of other artists and face repeated exposure of their art and craft to strangers. Though many people like occasional experiences onstage, the discipline, skill, and control required of the professional performer require special dedication. The development of these skills usually requires private lessons or work at a conservatory combined with practice in the field. Experience performing is the only way to learn whether it is for you. Working for a few years in repertory theater, performing in clubs or at private parties, volunteering to sing in a chorus, or working in any way possible on the stage will help you decide whether to pursue a career in the field. If you want to become a performer it is also essential to find a community of performers to work with and learn from.

C. Direction

Directing a work is a complex and distinct skill. The director puts a performance together and renders an interpretation of it. The creator and the performer are mediated by the director and as a consequence that role requires many different skills and considerable experience. However, directors always need help, ranging from people to get them a cup of coffee or hold a script or keep a diary of the development of a production. Young people interested in directing should try their hand at it on an amateur level, perhaps as a volunteer working in schools with young children, and then be willing to spend time as a gofer. As in many other forms of work, getting access to the place of work is one of the most crucial steps and sometimes requires beginning with very menial work.

D. Design

Design plays a pervasive role in the arts and media. Designers create the basic pattern for performances and exhibits: the sets and costumes of a play; the look and decor of a theater or gallery or museum; the typeface, look, and size of a book; the logo a company or person uses for identification; the nature of display cases, bookshelves, coffee cups, tables and desks, and the decor of rooms or homes; the landscape of a park or garden; frames for paintings and the display windows in stores; costumes and the spaceships and monsters used in movie special effects.

Designers can be self-trained or take design classes in college or at art schools. Some people begin their design careers doing floor and window displays in local department stores; others work on theater sets or in wood and metal shops that have resident designers. Landscape designers frequently hire young people to carry out their designs, and they can be good teachers. Environmental designers occasionally have commissions to design and supervise the building of parks and playgrounds. Working on a building project also provides an opportunity to get to know something about a designer's work.

E. Technical Crafts

Technical crafts range all the way from electronics and computer control of systems to sound and light technology. Carpentry and machine skills, as well as knowledge of motors, engines, plastics, and fabric, are all used in the arts and media. It is easier to break into a working artistic environment with those skills than if you come in cold. Manual and mechanical skills are easy to acquire at community colleges, and it makes sense to learn in addition how to design and build things, even if you won't use those skills on an everyday basis in your work.

F. Editorial

Editors are internal critics, people who advise artists and critique their work in the spirit of making it better. They are different than professional critics, who evaluate the final product for newspapers and magazines, and who are often adversaries of artists and performers.

Good editors do not necessarily have to be artists themselves, though a number are. They have to be knowledgeable and sensitive to the nuances of creation and the quality of artistic work. If you love an art and yet don't feel you have the desire or talent to be an artist, editorial work can be a very rewarding option.

G. Criticism

Criticism is a difficult, sensitive craft that requires a great deal of knowledge and highly tuned senses and sensibilities. It is not easy to write good criticism, and if you want to do it, you should become immersed in as much of the art you want to write about as possible. It is also important to read journals, newspapers, and books of criticism and to write essays and reviews of your own.

It also doesn't hurt to submit reviews to local papers and to write to established critics and ask them for advice on how you should go about becoming a critic.

H. Production

Producing involves putting an entire artistic or media package together. This includes, but isn't limited to, raising money; contacting and working with the artists, director, and performers (if there are any); getting a venue to exhibit or perform; coordinating publicity and sales, and in general having the overall responsibility to see that everything involved is done well. Youngsters who produce rock or reggae shows, or who take charge of putting on school plays or dances, have small-scale experience in producing.

Producers love volunteers, because they often need help with details and welcome people who can do tedious and repetitive small tasks with good humor. An advantage of working with a producer is that you get a sense of how all the aspects of a production work together.

I. Administration

Administration of arts-and-media-related activity requires business and accounting skills as well as specific knowledge of the special organizational and financial structures of artistic work. It also helps to know about nonprofit organizations because many arts groups are incorporated as nonprofit corporations. For someone who likes to keep things organized and running efficiently, arts businesses are interesting places to work.

J. Publicity and Sales

Publicity and sales provide interesting challenges. How do you get people to know about an event, and how do you get them to come? The work ranges from getting posters made and distributed to setting up radio and TV interviews, book signings, speeches, and other publicity events. It requires getting to know people in the media, artists, and other promoters, as well as public relations people, and advertising agencies. Working in publicity requires a combination of charm and aggression and a delight in being in the company of people. It is not a role for shy and retiring people, but can be an extrovert's dream.

K. Running a Venue

Running an exhibition or performance center such as a movie theater, live performance theater, exhibition gallery, or museum requires management skills and taste. It involves all of the skills necessary to keep a place clean, efficient, and technically sound. It also involves selecting programs, at times managing the integration of performance with food and drink, dealing with band managers and booking agents, bargaining over fees and admission costs, ordering food, and making sure that details such as clean tablecloths and bathrooms are taken care of. People who own and run venues always need help, and if you can put up with all of the details that have to be taken care of, being a club or gallery manager can be very exciting because it gives you the opportunity to "discover" talent and determine, to a degree, current styles in the arts.

L. Manager/Agent

Being a manager, agent, or broker of artists' talents is another way to be involved in the arts. The agent or broker takes the responsibility for getting shows and booking performances and has to go back and forth between the artists and the people who run the venues, as well as the producers. A good agent can promote mediocre talent or nurture genius.

The usual route to becoming an agent or manager is through apprenticing yourself to an established agent or manager, or by managing some of your friends and winging it for a while until you meet people in the business and get a feel for how things work.

M. Manufacturing

Manufacturing posters, records, art reproductions, furniture, jewelry, ceramics, and household fixings, as well as developing and duplicating films, photographs, and videos, casting sculptures, and publishing books, are all part of the arts and media industry. Many small plants require skilled work and will train people. They are worth exploring.

Areas of Work

A. Writing

There are many different forms of writing, and high school students usually have experience with only a few of them. On page 198 is a list of twelve fairly distinct types of writing, each of which leads to a different career, though some writers do many different types of commercial writing in order to support their own creative writing. Notice that there are a number of blank lines at the bottom of the list. If you think of some forms of writing that have been left out, just add them on those lines. (In fact, all of the profile forms in this book can be looked on as open-ended grids. You should feel free to add to them and modify them to fit your own needs and perceptions.)

Sample Writing Profiles

Each type of writing has its own conventions and outlets. For example, poetry, advertising, business reports, and technical writing do not take the same form and are not published

TYPES OF WRITING

1. JOURNALISM
2. POETRY AND FICTION
3. FILM, THEATER
4. ADVERTISING
5. REVIEWING AND FEATURE WRITING
6. BUSINESS REPORTS
7. PROPOSALS / FUND-RAISING
8. EDUCATIONAL MATERIALS
9. SPEECHWRITING
10. TECHNICAL WRITING
11. TV, RADIO
12. NONFICTION (PROSE)
13. _____
14. _____
15. _____

in the same way. When you decide to do a particular kind of writing you also commit yourself to working within a particular world where that writing has an audience. Therefore, if you choose to explore a career in writing, it makes sense to look through the list of types of writing first and consider several types of writing before completing the full profile.

Here are two sample profiles, one done by a high school junior and the other by a senior who for a while has been determined to be a writer but had no idea how to focus her dreams.

Phillip

Phillip likes politics but is very shy. He's curious about business but he's not aggressive. He loves to read nonfiction, especially history, economics, and politics. However, he doesn't want to be a historian, economist, businessman, or politician. He would like to do something with writing that involves getting to know people in business and economics and would also like to learn to write both for and about those people. When he had finished marking his copy of the types of writing list, it looked like this:

· · · · · · · · · · · · · · · · · ·

TYPES OF WRITING

1. JOURNALISM
2. POETRY AND FICTION
3. FILM, THEATER
4. ADVERTISING
5. REVIEWING AND FEATURE WRITING
✓ 6. BUSINESS REPORTS
7. PROPOSALS / FUND-RAISING
8. EDUCATIONAL MATERIALS
✓ 9. SPEECHWRITING
10. TECHNICAL WRITING
11. TV, RADIO
✓ 12. NONFICTION (PROSE)
13. _____
14. _____
15. _____

Phillip's Chart

Phillip indicated that he would like to write nonfiction (mostly history and biography), speeches, and business reports. His long-range goal was to write books about politics and political and business leaders. He filled out the rest of the WORK IN MEDIA AND THE ARTS profile form as shown on the following page.

Phillip wants to be a writer, not an editor or critic or publisher. He also wants to be involved with a corporation that has in-house writers or contracts with free-lance writers for reports, newsletters, and other publications; with a college that has good history and economics departments; and with a political organization where he might be able to work with a speechwriter. He's willing to do anything from typing to making coffee in order to learn how speeches are actually created in a political situation where their content is carefully scrutinized.

Since Phillip is a junior in high school, he said he would like to take advantage of his high school's independent study program and take a course in contemporary politics at the local

·

WORK IN MEDIA AND THE ARTS

Areas of Work	Modes	Places of Work	Ways You Can Become Involved
A. Writing	A. Creation	A. Studio	A. Volunteer work
B. TV and radio	B. Performance		B. Summer work
C. Film and video	C. Direction	B. Business	
D. Photography	D. Design		C. Apprenticeships
E. Music	E. Technical crafts	C. College/school	
F. Theater	F. Editorial		D. Entry-level work
G. Dance	G. Criticism	D. Community center	
H. Fiber arts and fashion	H. Production		E. Semiskilled and skilled work
I. Painting and printmaking	I. Administration	E. Home	
J. Sculpture and 3-dimensional art	J. Publicity and sales		F. Independent study
K. Industrial and commercial design	K. Running a venue	F. Organizations	
L. Jewelry, glass, and ceramics	L. Manager/agent	G. TV/radio network or station	
M. Crafts	M. Manufacturing	H. Theater	
		I. Production center	
		J. Craft fairs	

Phillip's Profile

junior college while pursuing volunteer work at the office of the local Democratic party or at some corporation. He has the summer free and is willing to volunteer his time.

Phillip's lucky in that he has a semester during his junior year in high school, his whole senior year in high school, and two summers to explore his particular interests in writing. He plans to use the rest of his high school career writing and learning about the world of business and politics. Then he hopes to go on to college and study history and writing while continuing to volunteer (or, he hopes, work) using his writing skills in politics and business. He also intends to keep a journal of his experiences with the idea that it might be useful for future writing.

Jill

Jill is a senior in the last semester of high school. She also wants to explore writing as a career. The chart of her writing preferences appears on the following page.

Jill wants to write poetry and children's fiction as well as educational textbooks. She has written poetry and wrote a story

·

. . . .

TYPES OF WRITING

1. JOURNALISM
✓ 2. POETRY AND FICTION
3. FILM, THEATER
4. ADVERTISING
5. REVIEWING AND FEATURE WRITING
6. BUSINESS REPORTS
7. PROPOSALS / FUND-RAISING
✓ 8. EDUCATIONAL MATERIALS
9. SPEECHWRITING
10. TECHNICAL WRITING
11. TV, RADIO
12. NONFICTION (PROSE)
13. _____
14. _____
15. _____

Jill's Chart

for her twelve-year-old sister, who loved it and urged her to write more. She told me that her poetry was very personal and that she felt she could learn how to hone her skills by reading and getting to meet and talk with other poets. She attends poetry readings and has been able to find people willing to read and criticize her work.

The profile Jill filled out, which is shown on the following page, is a bit complex. She wants to create poetry and children's books as well as produce educational materials. She is also interested in performance—that is, in reading her poetry for audiences and reading and telling stories at schools and community centers. She'd like to hook up with a poetry program or artist-in-the-schools program, or with a school that takes volunteers or has a small budget for the arts. Actually, her sister's school has expressed an interest in having her work part-time there.

She likes writing at home and would like to work in a book-

WORK IN MEDIA AND THE ARTS

Areas of Work	Modes	Places of Work	Ways You Can Become Involved
A. Writing	A. Creation	A. Studio	A. Volunteer work
B. TV and radio	B. Performance		
C. Film and video	C. Direction	B. Business	B. Summer work
D. Photography	D. Design		
E. Music	E. Technical crafts	C. College/school	C. Apprenticeships
F. Theater	F. Editorial		
G. Dance	G. Criticism	D. Community center	D. Entry-level work
H. Fiber arts and fashion	H. Production		
I. Painting and printmaking	I. Administration	E. Home	E. Semiskilled and skilled work
J. Sculpture and 3-dimensional art	J. Publicity and sales	F. Organizations	F. Independent study
K. Industrial and commercial design	K. Running a venue	G. TV/radio network or station	
L. Jewelry, glass, and ceramics	L. Manager/agent	H. Theater	
M. Crafts	M. Manufacturing		
		I. Production center	
		J. Craft fairs	

Jill's Profile

store (the venue) and learn how to become a bookstore manager. One reason she wants a job at a bookstore is that she wants to be around books and have a chance to look at all of the current work she can't afford to buy. Another is that she knows of some bookstores that employ young writers and she would like to become part of a community of writers.

After looking at the profile, Jill began to order her priorities for the year after high school. Her tentative list looked like this:

1. Try to get job at bookstore.
2. Volunteer or get work at school.
3. Go over old writing and start new work.
4. Ask people how you get on a poetry-reading program.
5. Find educational and poetry publishers.

Jill decided to begin to do these things before graduation and, realizing it would take time to find the right places, to give herself the whole summer to explore opportunities. She decided to worry about college halfway through the next year and feels confident that she will discover the right way to become a writer.

Note: I broke down the category of writing into many subcategories. The same can be done for the rest of the entries in this column of the profile form, each of which is broad enough to merit its own book. I've only included some of the most salient features of these areas. However, in the Appendix at the end of this book you will find references to books that deal with careers in media and the arts. These books provide useful, detailed overviews of different types of work and give useful references to yet other books, and to state and nationwide resources. However, to make contacts closer to home, the Yellow Pages and your personal contacts still provide a good focused beginning.

B. TV and Radio

There are national TV and radio networks, as well as community and college-based stations. It is very difficult, if not impossible, for a young person to find a way to work or volunteer on the network level. However, it is easier to find a place at local public radio stations and at some local commercial stations as well.

If you want to go into either TV or radio you should think through what specific aspect you want to work in. For example, are you interested in doing news, or sports, or features, or sitcoms? Do you want to become involved with quiz shows, or music shows, or with the production of commercials?

To choose to become involved with TV or radio is just a first step. You then have to begin to break down your choice into the specific subareas that people work in. Of course, you're not limited to choosing only one very specific area, such as made-for-TV dramatic one-hour movies. But the greater the focus you have, the easier it will be to discover the people you should contact.

In the area of TV and radio, it helps to be very literate about the medium. That implies doing a lot of listening, viewing, reading, and visiting before breaking on the scene and presenting yourself. Pick a local station and hang out there if you want to break in.

C. Film and Video

There are many small and medium-size independent filmmakers who make everything from business films, commercials, political films, TV films, cartoons, and other animated works, to filmstrips, educational films, travelogues, and documentaries. It makes sense to think about the kind of films you would like to make before making contact with people in the business. Use the list of types of films to make an initial choice.

TYPES OF FILMS AND VIDEO

1. COMMERCIAL FILM (STORIES)
2. DOCUMENTARIES
3. ART AND EXPERIMENTAL
4. BUSINESS FILMS
5. EDUCATIONAL FILMS
6. TRAVELOGUES
7. ADS, COMMERCIALS, MUSIC VIDEOS
8. ANIMATION
9. TV FEATURES AND NEWS
10. _____

· · · · · · · · · · · · · · · · ·

This sampling taken from the Manhattan telephone book gives examples of the kinds of businesses one can find in most cities, and even in many small towns.

· – – – – **765-5170**	
NS	
– – – – –765-4646	
– – – – – 967-1510	

ısic Scoring

– – – – – –353-9468

Specialists
· – – – – 382-0220
· – – – – 697-9800
– – – – – 757-9400
· – – – – 586-0209
nc
– – – – –697-9800
4 E 49– – 751-2510

– – – – 921-0555

ɘs
– – – – 921-0555
– – – – 753-3234

:rap

ɪrvicing

· – – – – 764-4290
– – – – – 620-5654
)RP
– – – **718 784-4040**
– – – – –944-1788
– – – – – 944-1788

– – – 718 784-4040

'ing
– – – – – **265-0864**

tories

– – – – 730-0555
– – – – 247-3415
W 40– – 921-1299
– – – – 757-5622
– – – – –757-4580

– – – – –757-4580
– – – – 265-5530
– – – – –691-5613
– – – – 279-5438
· – – – – 302-7373
– – – – 977-8980

Cineric Inc 321 W 44 – – – – – – – – – – – 586-4822
Cynosure Films Inc 630 9 Av – – – – – – – – 245-1648
Exceptional Opticals Inc 28 W 39 – – – – – 840-3222
I F Studios Inc 15 W 38 – – – – – – – – – – 819-1880
Production Suites Inc 601 W 50 – – – – – – 246-0501
Production Suites Inc 601 W 50 – – – – – – 246-9407

▶ **Motion Picture Producers & Studios**

A B Cine Inc 137 E 25 – – – – – – – – – – – 683-3440
A Major Studios Inc 342 Mad Av – – – – – – 697-8503
A & R Group 30 W 26 – – – – – – – – – – – 989-2366
Abacab Prodctns Inc 123 W 44 – – – – – – 575-3108
Abele Micki Prodctns 236 W 26 – – – – – – 675-8916
ACM Prodctns 306 W 38 – – – – – – – – – – 947-3699
Action Prodctns Inc 14 E 39 – – – – – – – – 684-4250
Actors In Advtng 39 W 19 – – – – – – – – – 645-0030
Admaster Inc 95 Mad Av – – – – – – – – – – 679-1134
Aegis Prodctns Inc 144 E 39 – – – – – – – – 684-0810
Albert Ruddy Productions 340 W 57 – – – – 247-0488
Allan Albert Inc 55 Greene – – – – – – – – 989-1572
Allan Albert Inc 530 W 23 – – – – – – – – – 627-1590
American Film Technology Inc
  555 Mad Av – – – – – – – – – – – – – – – 838-7933
American Motion Picture Co Inc
  159 W 53 – – – – – – – – – – – – – – – – 586-1731
Animated Prodctns Inc 1600 Bway – – – – 265-2942
Anomaly Films 135 Hudson – – – – – – – – 925-1500
Arc Films Inc 7 W 18 – – – – – – – – – – – 627-3336
Armstrong Information Svces Inc
  141 E 44 – – – – – – – – – – – – – – – – 986-0910
Artvision 140 E 81 – – – – – – – – – – – – – 472-2373
Astor Realty Corp 322 W 57 – – – – – – – – 397-3565
Atelier Cinema Video Stages 295 W 4 – – – 243-3550
Atl Call – – – – – – – – – – – – – – – – – – 243-3577
Aten & Co 140 W 69 – – – – – – – – – – – – 496-5560
Atlantic Motion Picturer Inc 162 W 21 – – – 924-6170
Atlantic Releasing Corp 475 Park Av S – – – 213-3232
Auchincloss Gordon 439 E 51 St – – – – – – 753-0320
August Films Inc 321 W 44 – – – – – – – – – 582-7025
Avon Prodctns 511 W 54 – – – – – – – – – – 581-4460
B C Studios 152 W 25 – – – – – – – – – – – 242-4065
Ball & Chain 151 W 28 – – – – – – – – – – – 629-0808
BALSMEYER & EVERETT INC
  230 W 17 – – – – – – – – – – – – – – – – **627-3430**
Baxter Films Inc 260 5 Av – – – – – – – – – 532-4700
Beckerman Howard 25 W 45 – – – – – – – – 869-0595
Beeman Prodctns 385 Canal – – – – – – – – 334-5273
Ben-Lar Prodctns Inc 311 W 24 – – – – – – 255-5553
BERGMAN LESTER V & ASSOCS INC
  Inserts, Science, Microscopy, Agri
  225 E Mountn Rd S Cld Sp – – – – – – – 914 265-3656
Bernadell Inc P O Box 1897 Old Chelsea Sta – 463-7000
Berner Fred 466 Washngtn – – – – – – – – – 219-3210
Bert Steinhauser Prodctn Inc 23 E 22 – – – 477-1377
Bianchi Films Inc 141 5 Av – – – – – – – – – 505-0670
Big Apple Releasing Inc 15 W 26 – – – – – – 685-1322

Blackwood Christiː
  115 Bank – – – – –
BLECHMAN R O IN
  2 W 47 – – – – – –
Blue Gander Inc 1(
Blue Mountain Filɾ
Bluebird Films 165
Blumenthal David
Bob Ahrens Prodcˑ
BOB THOMAS PRO
  Motion Picture ˌ
  60 E 42 – – – – –
Bon Bon Enterpris
Boulevard Commn
Brainstorm Produc
Brane Prodctn Inc
Brett Productions
Brillig Prodctns Inɾ
Bruce Van Dusen
Buckholtz Tom Prˌ
Budin Elbert 424 W
BUDIN ELBERT
  424 W 33 – – – –
Bunin Elinor Prodˌ
CAMERA MART ST
  Rentals, Camerˌ
  Editing
  See Our Displaˌ
  456 W 55 – –
Carousel Film Inc
Cel-Art Prodctns ꞁ
Century III Teleproˌ
  651 Beacon Bostoɾ
Chal Productions
Chappell-Sonnenfˌ
CHARISMA PRODˌ
Cherub Films Inc ˌ
Chester For Co Inˌ
Chiasma Prodctns
Chrome Yellow Fil
Cine International
Cine-Metric Inc 2ˌ
Cinema Arts Assoˌ
Cinema Mistral 55
Cinemakers Inc 3ˌ
City Lights Prodctˌ
Claiborne William
Coane Prodctns Iɾ
Coast To Coast Pɾ
Cogent Communiˌ
Cohen Charles 52ꞁ
Collective For Livɪ
Colman Group Thˌ
COLUMBIA PICTUˌ
  711 5 Av – – – –
Columbia Pictures
Columbia Pictures

. . . .

A number of large studios and independent film producers also exist, of course, but it's hard to get into them without having some prior experience.

It makes sense to explore the field of film by finding a way to make your own videos and going to a film museum or archive and looking at as many films as you can. In addition, ask people at the museum or archive about local filmmakers, and look them up. Watch the newspaper for announcements of film openings where the filmmakers will talk to the audience.

Also remember that there are many different ways to work in film and that there are film jobs that fit every category in the "Modes" column on the profile form. If you are interested in finding out what those jobs are, as an exercise, write down all the credits on the next film you see and then get a book on film from the library that will tell you just what the people with those different jobs do.

D. Photography

Photography is one field that is easy to break into. All you need is a camera (35 mm is best), film, a developing tank for black-and-white film, and a good eye. You can start at home by taking family pictures and offering to take pictures at birthday and anniversary parties, dances, and other celebrations. It's possible to start out by doing this for the cost of color film and developing. Also ask for an extra set of your pictures you can keep. Take the best of these pictures and build up a portfolio you can share at some later date with a professional photographer who can offer you constructive criticism—or even a job.

Another way to break into photography is to take pictures of local school and community events (in black and white) and persistently submit them to a local newspaper. After a while you'll probably find yourself getting published. When you are, be sure the paper gives you a photo credit under the shot. On page 207 is a list of some common types of photography.

E. Music

There is no limit to the forms and genres of music. Once you have an idea of the types of music you would like to

.

. . . .

TYPES OF PHOTOGRAPHY

1. NEWS
2. SPORTS
3. DOCUMENTARY
4. PORTRAIT
5. LANDSCAPE AND ANIMAL
6. TRAVEL
7. ART
8. INDUSTRIAL
9. FASHION
10. ADVERTISING
11. AERIAL
12. _____

become involved in, fill out the profile form. The musicians' union, ASCAP, music schools, and conservatories are sources of information, as are performers and technicians you can meet after performances if you hang around. Other excellent sources of information about music as a career are music store clerks, many of whom are practicing musicians themselves.

Volunteering to do mechanical and manual labor for musicians or to help a theater or club with its setup is one way to make contacts and get a feel for how people break into music.

Finding a good teacher is essential for performers and composers. Once again, music store clerks are often good sources of suggestions for teachers.

F. Theater

There are many different types of live theater, and there are also many different ways to become involved in play production. For example, the following positions (in addition to actors) were listed on a playbill I got from a local commercial repertory theater: director, set designer, properties designer, costume designer, lighting technician and designer, musical director, composer, dance consultant, vocal coach, stage manager, assistant stage manager, producer, publicity director, and scenic technician. If you want to be in the theater, you can usually find a way as long as you are not obsessed with the idea of beginning as a star.

G. Dance

There are many different forms of dance, and these usually require different types of training (though not a college degree). Ballet requires strict discipline and structured training from an early age. Modern ballet, acrobatic dancing, and show dancing also require lessons, though they may not initially demand as much of the dancer. However, no matter what form of dancing one chooses, the choice of dancing as a career requires full dedication to honing one's physical and musical skills. It is not a choice to be made lightly, and it is probably a good idea to consult local teachers, find someone at a ballet company or dance troupe to audition for, and in general be careful and thorough about finding training and creating opportunities for performance.

H. Fiber Arts and Fashion

Fiber arts range from spinning, rug making, weaving, and knitting, to quilting, crocheting, and making sculpted fiber works. They also include loom making, dyeing, batiking, and textile design. The products of fiber arts are, to name just a few, sweaters, jackets, dresses, upholstery, curtains, rugs, flags, sculptures, scarves, tablecloths, and wall hangings.

There are a number of small weaving studios that turn out commercial fiber works, and many weavers work at home. These studios and a number of home weavers also teach. It is possible to learn weaving and its allied arts through them or at any number of art centers and schools.

In addition, there are large commercial textile manufacturers who work from weavers' designs and mechanize the entire process of weaving. Fabric designers and fashion designers often work together.

Fashion design can be learned at school or through becoming an apprentice to a designer. Many boutiques are run by designers, and if you're interested in the field, you might visit local ones, chat with people about their work, and try to get a temporary job.

I. Painting and Printmaking

If you are interested in painting, drawing, etching, lithography, monoprinting, or other forms of graphics, it makes sense to send away for catalogs from art colleges. These catalogs will give you an idea of the kinds of classes art students take, and an inkling of the kind of skills that are demanded of them.

Arts businesses, which produce graphics ranging from posters, book and magazine illustrations, comic books, postcards, greeting cards, murals, and ads, are listed in the Yellow Pages. There are also a number of books on the different types of careers one can have that are related to graphic arts, some of which are listed in the Appendix.

Some people might choose to go straight to art school after high school, but many potentially gifted artists do not get the training in high school that would get them into a good art academy or college. Nevertheless, many schools and art classes can prepare one for an art career or for art school. It's worth taking a year to get one's skills together while taking classes, spending time at museums, and, if possible, volunteering in a gallery or as a docent or museum guide. Framing shops or art supply stores are also possible work sites. The essential thing is to find out where the artists are and find a way to talk to people who are doing what you would like to do.

J. Sculpture and Three-Dimensional Art

The things discussed in the section on painting and printmaking apply to sculpture and three-dimensional art as well. But in addition, you should learn as many as possible of the

sculpturing skills needed for wood and stone carving, clay mod-
eling, welding, and other forms of metalwork. In addition,
knowledge of motors and engines, electronics, and sound and
light are useful skills for the sculptor.

While acquiring these skills (many of which are taught at
vocational schools or community art centers) it makes sense to
try your hand at sculpting and to visit foundries and sculptors'
studios if possible. Find out if any public sculpture is being
done and find ways to meet the people working on the projects.
Volunteer physical labor is often welcome in the world of
sculpture.

K. Industrial and Commercial Design

Designers create the look and feel of everything from sun-
glasses to milk cartons, furniture, household fixings, industrial
machines, jewelry, tools, games, and toys. Many design firms
specialize in one area of design or another, and many corporations have their own design departments, though many of the
skills needed to be a designer can best be acquired at a design
school or college that has a design or industrial design department. However, before investing time attending one of these
schools, it is a good idea to visit many design firms and volunteer or apprentice at one for a summer or a year. If you do go
on to design school, your work experience will make it easier
to master school-related skills.

L. Jewelry, Glass, and Ceramics

Work in jewelry, glass, and ceramics can be very simple; it
can also be incredibly complex and demand very exacting skills.
Basic skills in these arts can be acquired at home or at a craft
school, but as soon as one starts casting metal jewelry and setting stones, blowing and shaping glass, or throwing and glazing
complicated pots and ceramic sculptures, studio work is necessary. Physical work is a given. Apprenticeships in these particular arts are usually available because many good teachers
work in the studio all of the time.

There are many galleries and shops that show and sell jewelry, blown and stained glass, and ceramics. If you take a tour

of shops and galleries you'll usually find business cards of many of the artists, and if you're not shy, call them up and ask them how you can get involved. In addition, go to ceramic, glass, and jewelry supply stores. They usually have bulletin boards with calling cards and announcements for studio work, lessons, apprenticeships, and jobs.

M. Crafts

One way to discover the range and variety of crafts work is to go to a craft fair. Most likely you'll find candles, dolls, inexpensive stained glass, some ceramics, handcrafted wooden toys and furniture, lots of costume jewelry and maybe even some one-of-a-kind artistic jewelry, handmade and printed stationery, knitted and woven scarves and sweaters, tie-dyed T-shirts, and many other items that can be made at home by one to a few people. Many fairs even specify that they will not allow people to sell items they didn't make.

Most craft work begins with some traditional folk form and is varied by the craftsperson. If you like to travel, are willing to spend hours making some craft item, and have a way of giving your work a unique personality, it's possible to make a modest living on the fair circuit. It's also possible to make retail contacts at the fairs. Many people eventually get off the circuit and set up small businesses that supply their work to enough retail outlets to give them a modest income.

Some Sample Profiles

Here are some sample profiles and a few exercises in the development of profiles in media and the arts. You may want to skip over them at this point and go on to the next chapter. On the other hand, if you'd like a bit of practice in profile interpretation, you may find them of value.

Kate

After looking over the WORK IN MEDIA AND THE ARTS profile, Kate said she always thought of becoming a photographer and might like to spend a year trying it out. I showed her the list of types of photography, and she immediately chose portrait and landscape and animal photography. She said she loved to take pictures of people. She also loved to photograph animals, plants, and stone formations. It turned out she had two scrapbooks full of her favorite photographs, a 35-mm camera, and a Polaroid.

TYPES OF PHOTOGRAPHY

1. NEWS
2. SPORTS
3. DOCUMENTARY
✔ 4. PORTRAIT
✔ 5. LANDSCAPE AND ANIMAL
6. TRAVEL
7. ART
8. INDUSTRIAL
9. FASHION
10. ADVERTISING
11. AERIAL
12. _____

Kate's Chart

Kate and I went over the entries in the profile form and I suggested she take it home for a few days and think about how she might like to fill it in. The result is on page 213.

Kate is not one for simple options. Her choices reflected a basic strength she has: the ability to do many projects at the same time without compromising the quality of the work.

The idea she came up with for the summer after high school was to get a picture-taking booth at some local fairs and sell Polaroid photos of people dressed up in costumes she would

·

. . . .

WORK IN MEDIA AND THE ARTS

Areas of Work	Modes	Places of Work	Ways You Can Become Involved
A. Writing	A. Creation	A. Studio	A. Volunteer work
B. TV and radio	B. Performance		B. Summer work
C. Film and video	C. Direction	B. Business	
D. Photography	D. Design		C. Apprenticeships
E. Music	E. Technical crafts	C. College/school	
F. Theater	F. Editorial		D. Entry-level work
G. Dance	G. Criticism	D. Community center	
H. Fiber arts and fashion	H. Production		E. Semiskilled and skilled work
I. Painting and printmaking	I. Administration	E. Home	
J. Sculpture and 3-dimensional	J. Publicity and		F. Independent study
art	sales	F. Organizations	
K. Industrial and commercial	K. Running a venue		
design	L. Manager/agent	G. TV/radio network or station	
L. Jewelry, glass, and ceramics	M. Manufacturing		
M. Crafts		H. Theater	
		I. Production center	
		J. Craft fairs	

Kate's Profile

provide. She had done that before at a benefit for her brother's school and knew just how to set things up. In addition, she felt she could set up a photography business at home and do wedding, anniversary, and school photographs during the year. The fair was just for summer fun and a bit of experience.

Kate also hoped to take classes in photography at the local art museum and to find a local film-processing business that did customized printing and enlarging. She didn't want to work for minimum wage at a twenty-four-hour developing shop, where you never found out how to control the process. Her idea was to find a place where she could gain technical skills while working or helping out as an apprentice. She had two places in mind, both of which did photo processing for industry and magazines. She is currently exploring those options.

Jules
Jules said he didn't have the slightest idea what he wanted to do with his life. The only things he liked were skateboarding

.

2 1 3

and quality comic books, of which he had quite a valuable collection. He was a senior in high school and didn't want to go on to college, though his parents were pressuring him to go and not just hang around. Jules resisted them primarily because of the experiences of two of his skateboarding friends who went off to college the previous year—one dropped out immediately and the other was bored. They both advised Jules to do anything but go to college.

It is, of course, possible that Jules might find something inspiring at college. One never knows, and the best parents can do is provide their children with as many options as possible and try to help them choose the routes that seem the most fulfilling at this particular stage of their life.

Jules's parents suggested he fill out one of the profile forms anyway, and he chose WORK IN MEDIA AND THE ARTS. He decided two areas of work might interest him. Here's his profile:

WORK IN MEDIA AND THE ARTS

Areas of Work	Modes	Places of Work	Ways You Can Become Involved
A. Writing	A. Creation	A. Studio	A. Volunteer work
B. TV and radio	B. Performance		B. Summer work
C. Film and video	C. Direction	B. Business	
D. Photography	D. Design	C. College/school	C. Apprenticeships
E. Music	E. Technical crafts		D. Entry-level work
F. Theater	F. Editorial	D. Community center	
G. Dance	G. Criticism		E. Semiskilled and skilled work
H. Fiber arts and fashion	H. Production	E. Home	
I. Painting and printmaking	I. Administration		F. Independent study
J. Sculpture and 3-dimensional art	J. Publicity and sales	F. Organizations	
K. Industrial and commercial design	K. Running a venue	G. TV/radio network or station	
L. Jewelry, glass, and ceramics	L. Manager/agent	H. Theater	
M. Crafts	M. Manufacturing	I. Production center	
		J. Craft fairs	

Jules's Profile

Jules chose "Painting and printmaking" and explained that what he meant to choose was working on the art in comic books and on posters. He didn't want to create the stories or draw the figures. He wanted to do coloring, inking in the pencil drawings, and layout. The other thing he said he might be interested in was working at a factory where stained-glass windows and hangings were assembled. A friend of his had worked at one and Jules loved to visit it.

Jules also indicated that he didn't feel he deserved a job working in those areas because he had no skill. He was willing to work at a local fast-food place if he could get an apprenticeship with a local comic book studio or at the glass factory. But, he told his parents, there was no guarantee he'd like that kind of work or even that he'd try hard to do good work.

Jules had a lot of experience with school failure and I think he was preparing himself to fail again. His parents weren't enthusiastic about his choice, and the last I heard from them, they were still arguing over whether he should go to college or not. However, without telling his parents, he visited the stained-glass factory and was told that if he were willing to work for a while as a shipping clerk, they might find a way to take him on as an apprentice.

He took the job for the summer but his plans for next year are not yet set. It's not hard to say that it's probably better for him to be learning something at the factory than hanging out with his friends in college, getting by with a C− average, and working at skateboarding and beer drinking.

Profile Form 3:

ECOLOGICAL

AND

ENVIRONMENTAL

WORK

ECOLOGICAL AND ENVIRONMENTAL WORK

Focus of Work	Types of Work	Places of Work	Ways You Can Become Involved
A. Water	A. Research	A. Urban	A. Volunteer work
B. Land	B. Documentation	B. Rural	
C. Minerals	C. Communication	C. Wilderness	B. Summer work
D. Atmosphere	D. Advocacy	D. Laboratory	
E. Man-made goods	E. Care/maintenance	E. Advocacy group	C. Apprenticeships
	F. Recreation	F. Fund-raising organization	
F. Waste management	G. Emergency services	G. Government agency	D. Entry-level work
	H. Medical/health	H. Corporation	
G. Plants/trees	I. Conservation	I. Community group	E. Semiskilled and skilled work
H. Wildlife	J. Preservation	J. School/college	
I. Human ecology	K. Restoration	K. Museum	F. Independent study
	L. Recycling and disposal	L. The ``field''	
J. Energy	M. Agriculture		
	N. Aquaculture		
	O. Horticulture		

PROFILE FORM #3

ECOLOGICAL AND environmental work ranges from fire management in the national parks and the study of animals in the wild to working toward technical, social, and political solutions to the problems of disposal of hazardous wastes, the reduction of urban smog, the preservation of the ozone layer, and the elimination of acid rain. It can deal with preserving species on the verge of extinction, cleaning up after oil spills, and testing for pesticide damage, water pollution, and soil erosion. In addition, it deals with our energy future, the management of public lands, the recycling of waste, and the intelligent use of natural resources in manufacturing.

It is perhaps no exaggeration to claim that the central concern of ecological and environmental work is the future of the earth as a habitable and comfortable environment for the maintenance of life. Some of this work is done on a modest scale: taking care of state and national parks, developing museum and school programs to make people aware of environmental issues, raising funds to preserve a stand of trees, working on an ordinance to preserve open space, or protecting a pond from pollution. Some of the work is abstract and technical, such as developing alternatives to pesticides, inventing technology for nonpolluting energy sources, and studying whole ecosystems in order to find ways to maintain the balance of life within them. In addition, there is political, legal, medical, and communications work to be done to make it possible to legislate adequate funds for the preservation of the planet.

The field of environmental and ecological work involves a moral commitment to a healthy planet and can engage the time and energy of young people as an area that is growing and will have to grow if we are to persist on earth.

THE Ecological and Environmental Work PROFILE

The following is a summary of some of the options available in environmental management and ecology.

Focus of Work

A. Water
B. Land

Some people have a special affinity for water, and others for land. This may sound superficially odd, but think of the need some people have to sail, or surf, or swim. Other people are equally attracted to mountains, plains, or deserts. No one is completely indifferent to his environmental conditions.

When it comes to choosing a vocation, water and land can play a major role in determining people's choices. Some people have to "go to sea"; others need to "keep in touch with the land." Farming, hunting, fishing, and sailing are some of the earliest of human vocations. Environmental and ecological work provides many new opportunities in this century and the next to work with water and land.

If you have an affinity for working with water, you might focus your work on the preservation, restoration, and nondestructive human uses of oceans, seas, inland lakes, rivers, and man-made water systems (ranging from dams and aqueducts to urban waterworks). Or you might focus on rainfall and underground water sources.

If you have an affinity for working directly with the land, you'll discover there is work that needs to be done to prevent the degeneration and overexploitation of the plains, forests, deserts, mountains, and the tundra. There are places of heavy habitation that need sensible environmental planning, and others that are sparsely populated now that need to be protected from overdevelopment and exploitation of resources in the future. There also are challenges to keep wilderness areas ecologically intact.

If you want to work with land or water issues it makes sense to think about what type of land or water you want to focus on to begin with. Of course, the fields of soil and water analysis, geology, and hydraulics also deal with many of these issues.

.

. . . .

C. Minerals

The exploration of mineral deposits, and the distribution, exploitation, and use of minerals in manufacture, is essential to modern industrial society. Yet the use and exploitation of minerals generates the problems of land pollution, the destruction of animal and plant environments, the displacement of human communities, and the creation of polluting wastes that cannot be easily disposed of. The study of minerals and the way they are extracted and used involves knowing about geology, mining, smelting, surveying, mapmaking, engineering, and economics. It's also a social discipline, in that it involves knowing the communities that are affected, and knowing about the medical and psychological effects of mining and manufacture.

Many environmental organizations are working to develop sensitive policies for mineral development, and many local groups around the country are working to preserve communities and resources. Certain government agencies are charged with regulation and monitoring of mineral development for pollution and land devastation, and there are legislators who are charged with policy making and implementation. These groups are potential sources of environmental work involving many different skills and forms of knowledge. You might do anything from help with land and mineral surveys to office work in Washington, D.C., or a state capital (volunteering to work for congressional committees is, for example, a very good way to get a taste of governmental work). You might work within the government or with an environmental group, or become involved with the National Geologic Survey. It is also possible to get jobs or apprenticeships with mining and other mineral corporations, some of which are becoming increasingly sensitive to environmental issues.

D. Atmosphere

Atmospheric studies deal with the weather and with conditions, such as smog and the ozone layer, that affect the quality of life. You can get involved with studying, predicting, and broadcasting the weather in a number of ways. The National

Weather Service is one. The National Science Foundation has atmospheric study programs it supports, as does NASA. Information about atmospheric studies can also be obtained from training centers for air traffic controllers and from hot-air balloonist groups.

The work ranges from observation to data analysis and prediction. Indirectly related are the fields of disaster warning and control and other emergency services that involve atmospheric research and reports. And there are places in the remotest spots on earth that have weather and atmospheric monitoring stations where it might be possible to work for a while if solitude is an attractive option.

E. Man-made Goods
F. Waste Management

The manufacture of machines and goods for consumption involves the use of raw materials, the creation of a site for manufacturing, transportation to and from the site, the use of human labor, and the production of waste by-products of the manufacturing process. Ecological and environmental concerns range from the safety of working conditions and the quality of work and life for the workers to the efficient use of materials and the disposal of waste products. Unions, governmental organizations, environmental groups, and small environmental management corporations often deal with these issues. Many of them are willing to take on volunteers or apprentices because there is more work that needs to be done than there are people currently involved. One good source for information about how to get involved is professors who teach ecology and environmental management classes at local colleges. Another is the Washington, D.C., Yellow Pages under the listing "Environmental, Conservation, and Ecological Organizations."

G. Plants/Trees
H. Wildlife

There are groups that try to protect wildlife and plant environments, and others that try to restore damaged environments. There are others that do natural life surveys and try to preserve endangered species before it is too late. The World Wildlife Fund, the Audubon Society, the Sierra Club, and any number of other organizations can provide access to local groups that are doing active work in these areas. They also have information about international projects. It is possible to volunteer or get apprentice work at one of these groups, and it's also possible to find out from them the most sensible career routes to lifelong environmental work. (I've provided an extensive list of other organizations that deal with the environment, in the appendix.)

Many of these organizations have good education programs in which representatives are sent into the schools to teach environmental education. They also mount public campaigns for support; one way you might become involved and make contacts is to participate actively in one of these drives.

In addition, many small environmental centers serve school districts and provide seminars and residential environmental programs. They often have apprentice training programs that involve working to maintain the center and teaching visiting schoolchildren and teachers. You can find out about these centers from state offices of education, which usually have an environmental education section.

I. Human Ecology

Human ecology deals with questions involving the care and nurturance of human populations. This includes such major issues as food supply, population density, birth control, energy systems, and resource management. Much of the work in these areas is done on an international scale, and organizations such as the United Nations (in particular UNICEF, FAO [Food and Agriculture Organization], UNESCO, and WHO [World Health Organization]), Worldwatch Institute (1776 Massachusetts Avenue NW, Washington, DC 20036), and Oxfam (115 Broadway, Boston, MA 02116) sponsor and support groups that work in these fields. There are also development projects that are sponsored by the United States government that range from the

Peace Corps to Oxfam. In addition to development work, many church groups and organizations like the Red Cross and Salvation Army have international aid and relief projects. There are often significant roles young people can play in these projects and all of these organizations will provide information on request. You can find addresses for them in the directories listed on page 272 in the Appendix.

J. Energy

The exploration of alternate energy sources, such as wind, solar, and biogas energy, is growing. Many businesses and small laboratories are leading the way in developing them. Check your state's department of energy and your local library.

In addition, this list mentions political groups that oppose nuclear energy and the environmental pollution caused by oil and gas. Young people are always welcome to join, and it's a good way to find out whether you would like to work in the environmental movement.

Types of Work

A. Research

This can consist of doing epidemiological studies (finding incidences of certain behaviors or conditions, such as diseases, in a whole population), anthropological accounts of the structure of human groups, and studies of the incidences of particular life-forms in normal and pathological situations. It can also consist of studying the medical effects of pesticides and the environmental consequences of oil spills, as well as the technology of solar energy and wind generation. Much of this work requires professional training, though there are many apprenticeships and assistantships at the entry level for young people who don't have any formal training. Someone has to take the samples, do simple chemical testing, do survey research, and occasionally remain in residence to gather information for longitudinal studies at a site. Doing environmental research for a year or two can motivate some people to get professional training and continue their work on more complex levels.

B. Documentation

Documentation is a very important part of environmental and ecological work. Life-forms have to be described and conditions investigated. A case has to be made for saving a species or for claiming pollution. Investigations have to be conducted, mappings and surveys have to be done, and causes of damage have to be uncovered. There is a sense of adventure to this work, for environmental detectives are essential to making a case for preservation or conservation. Some of the jobs involved in this kind of work are cartographer, statistician, field interviewer, surveyor, chemical analyst, photographer, illustrator, naturalist, and technical writer.

C. Communication

Communication about research results and specific environmental problems is necessary in order to mobilize public support and raise money for environmental action. Government and private sources usually have to be convinced that environmental concerns cannot be ignored or action delayed.

Writers, photographers, graphic artists, filmmakers, speakers, and performers are all needed. Some of the work is technical, such as the writing of environmental impact reports. Other writing is more popular and consists of doing newspaper and magazine features, interviews, newsletters, and handouts. The same is true of photography and film, which can be the source of popular works and also of scientific documentation.

There is also a need for people who can speak to community groups and schools, appear on the media, and in any way possible educate the public. Some of this work is paid and some volunteered, but there is always a need for people who can produce statements and images that make the case for environmental awareness and care.

D. Advocacy

Advocacy for environmental causes can consist of appearing before city councils or state legislatures, dealing directly with polluters, or bringing lawsuits against parties to a case of pollution, pesticide abuse, or environmental devastation. It can also consist of helping draw up legislation or organizing demonstrations and benefits. Almost all organizations dedicated to assisting the environment play some advocacy role and always need help. Each of these organizations has volunteer and paid staff, novices and professionals. They are good training places for careers in environmentally related professions.

E. Care/Maintenance
F. Recreation
G. Emergency Services

Care and maintenance of wilderness areas and parks is done by the U.S. National Parks Service and the Forestry Service, as well as by local and state agencies such as parks and recreation departments, and bureaus of fish and wildlife. Some of these organizations are also responsible for the recreational use of public lands. The U.S. National Parks Service has summer jobs for park guides and maintenance workers that high school graduates qualify for. There are also local jobs to be found in parks and at recreational facilities. Specific references for these jobs are listed in the Appendix of this book.

In addition, there is, unfortunately, always a need for emergency workers who are prepared to fight fires and floods, to clean up birds and fish after oil spills, help with hurricane and tornado damage, bring in emergency food supplies, and deal with evacuations. The Red Cross and Salvation Army deal with many such emergency services, as do many federal and state organizations.

H. Medical/Health

Medical and health work can relate directly to environmental issues. There is a need for skilled people to care for animals

· ·

and birds who are victims of environmental disasters. For example, in the Appendix there is a list of Raptor Centers where people can help with and get training for treating birds that are the victims of oil spills and other forms of ground and water pollution.

There is also a need for medical assistance for victims of occupational health hazards such as brown lung and black lung. Information about organizations that deal with health in the workplace can be obtained from the occupational health and safety administrations of the federal government and the states. Other sources of information are the health offices of unions.

Another form of environmental medicine is called epidemiology, which is the study of the incidence of different health conditions in a population. Epidemiological studies of the incidence of AIDS or malnutrition, for example, require many people to do survey research. An inquiry to the National Institutes of Health in Washington will provide information about local epidemiological studies, and if you are aggressive you might find a local study that will take you on.

Related to these studies are environmental monitoring projects. For example, there are many communities where ground-water pollution and radon levels are constantly checked, and your local department of health might have some positions for young people on these projects. There are also positions for people to help with emergency immunization and food programs. One good source of information about these programs is the UN's World Health Organization. Schools of public health may also be able to provide useful leads into this area.

I. Conservation
J. Preservation
K. Restoration
L. Recycling and Disposal

Conservation consists of the careful, nonwasteful management of existing resources; preservation is the saving of species or environments that are at risk; and restoration is the attempt to restore a damaged environment to a healthy state. All three activities require a lot of hard, concentrated work, as well as knowledge about the interactions of life-forms and environmental conditions. Specific projects throughout the world do all of these things, and many environmental groups, such as Friends of the Earth, the Sierra Club, and the Audubon Society, can refer you to them. Often there is an opportunity to travel associated with these activities.

Recycling can be done at home and in even the smallest communities. On a large scale, recycling projects are very important in the total maintenance of a nonpolluted environment. On a local level one can get involved in specific recycling and cleanup campaigns and even raise money for environmental campaigns by collecting recyclable glass and paper and selling it. Most towns have companies that buy recyclables, and you can find out about them through your state's Department of the Environment or through a local college's department of environmental studies. It's also possible to join the Conservation Corps and take part in brush and stream cleanups.

Waste disposal presents one of the major challenges people have to face these days. Plastics are not biodegradable, toxic chemicals don't go away, nuclear wastes are dangerous for hundreds of years, human waste pollutes water sources. Working on problems of waste management is more central to our long-range survival than one might imagine. It is a difficult yet worthwhile field. There are small research firms and government-supported groups working on these problems, as well as public advocacy groups that push for more resources to be allocated to cleanup and prevention.

M. Agriculture
N. Aquaculture
O. Horticulture

There is work to be done in farming and in raising sea life for food. The problems of chemicals in animal feed, the use of pesticides on fruit and vegetables, and the depletion and poisoning of certain species of fish and other sea life are central to the health of human and animal life and present a slightly different focus to agriculture. Organic farming, cleaning up streams and the oceans, the maintenance of fish breeding grounds, and the protection of shellfish life can all provide worthy work. A number of places are experimenting in fish management and organic agriculture, and working at one of these places for a year can introduce a teenager to the possibilities of careers in experimental farming.

In addition, it is possible to find work in horticulture ranging from growing and grafting plants in a nursery to getting involved in organic herb and flower truck gardening and working in landscaping.

The Appendix offers some places to contact for these different types of work.

Places of Work

The locations listed in the third column are self-explanatory, with the exception of the last listing: "The 'field.'" The "field" is the place where a project takes place. It may be in a wilderness area, a rural factory town, a city neighborhood, a remote mountain lookout, or an animal preserve. Many organizations have different field projects and it's possible to travel from one to another doing a specific type of work. People who work in the field are usually affiliated with a central organization and assigned to a field project.

Ways You Can Become Involved

The fourth column here is the same as it is in the other profile forms in the book.

After looking through the profile form, it might help you to look at several specific profiles and discuss ways of elaborating on them to gather resources and make contacts. Or you may want to skip over them for now and go on to the next chapter.

·

Elaborating on a Profile

Each one of the following completed profiles provides a sketch or outline of particular vocational affinities. However, without elaboration, most profiles don't provide enough information to gather appropriate resources. Take this simple environmental profile, which was generated by choosing the first entry in each of the four columns in the ECOLOGICAL AND ENVIRONMENTAL WORK profile form:

ECOLOGICAL AND ENVIRONMENTAL WORK

Focus of Work	Types of Work	Places of Work	Ways You Can Become Involved
A. Water	A. Research	A. Urban	A. Volunteer work
B. Land	B. Documentation	B. Rural	
C. Minerals	C. Communication	C. Wilderness	B. Summer work
D. Atmosphere	D. Advocacy	D. Laboratory	
E. Man-made goods	E. Care/maintenance	E. Advocacy group	C. Apprenticeships
	F. Recreation	F. Fund-raising organization	
F. Waste management	G. Emergency services	G. Government agency	D. Entry-level work
G. Plants/trees	H. Medical/health	H. Corporation	
H. Wildlife	I. Conservation	I. Community group	E. Semiskilled and skilled work
I. Human ecology	J. Preservation	J. School/college	
J. Energy	K. Restoration	K. Museum	F. Independent study
	L. Recycling and disposal	L. The "field"	
	M. Agriculture		
	N. Aquaculture		
	O. Horticulture		

Water Research Profile

Here's a verbal summary of this profile: volunteer research work dealing with water in an urban setting.

This summary is still not specific enough to enable one to decide what resources to gather and what people to contact. It's clear what "urban" and "volunteer" mean in this context, but "water" and "research" are more ambiguous. What are the roles of water in urban environments? And what research needs are there in this context?

First determine what you had in mind by choosing this profile. Sometimes the answer will simply be that it sounded interesting. There is no need to have a fully articulated vision in order to feel an affinity for a certain kind of vocation. In fact, the major points of using the profiles and elaborating on them are to allow for discovery and to slowly define, in increasingly specific ways, what you might like to do with your life. For that reason, expect a certain amount of ambiguity, uncertainty, disappointment, and the occasional abandonment of initial choices for a completely new and different profile to be central to the process.

In the instance at hand, it makes sense to start with "urban water" and, perhaps with your parents, make a list of all the ways in which water plays a role in urban life. Here's a partial list:

- drinking
- washing self, dishes, clothes
- sewage
- industrial usage
- air conditioning (cooling) and steam heating
- cleaning streets
- recreation (swimming, boating, etc.)

Now here are some factors relating to water usage that can lead to profile research:

- the treatment of water and its purity
- the adequacy of the sources
- the effects of bringing water to an urban setting
- contaminated water and its disposal
- the cost of water
- the system that transports water through the city
- the system that transports waste to points of disposal
- potentials for scarcity, effects of droughts, and preparations for emergency

These two lists lead to research questions such as:

- How pure is the water in a given city?
- How does purity get measured? How often?
- What is done when impurities or pollution are found?
- Does the water used for industry get recycled into the drinking water system?
- What is the effect of bringing water to the city upon the source communities and rivers, lakes, and dams?
- What emergency plans are there for disasters that might interrupt the water supply?

At this point you've collected enough specific information to elaborate on the initial profile in a number of different ways, according to your interests. Two examples are:

> **1.** I am interested in working with people who do research on the purity of drinking water in a city. I'd like to discover how purity is monitored and whether there are any sources of pollution coming from spills. I'm also interested in the recycling of industrially polluted water.
>
> **2.** I am interested in working with people who research the effects of bringing water into cities and who plan systems that carry water in and out of urban centers. I'm also interested in work that calculates how much water is needed and how the supply can be insured, as well as how emergencies are provided for.

Once you elaborate on your profile in this way, you'll find it is easier to search for places and people to contact. In the first case, one has to look for companies, government bureaus, and research laboratories that deal with water purity. In the second case, large-scale waterworks companies, dam builders, hydraulic engineers, planners, and emergency planning centers can all provide resources.

For both elaborations, one source of information would be government agencies; a few calls to local, county, state, and federal agencies would turn up some material. In addition, public utilities and waterworks would be good sources, as well as emergency organizations such as the Red Cross and Salvation Army. Universities have planning and engineering departments and their faculty can be a source for volunteer entry into fields involving urban water research. State departments of public health also have resources to offer.

Here's another ECOLOGICAL AND ENVIRONMENTAL WORK profile:

ECOLOGICAL AND ENVIRONMENTAL WORK

Focus of Work	Types of Work	Places of Work	Ways You Can Become Involved
A. Water	A. Research	A. Urban	A. Volunteer work
B. Land	B. Documentation	B. Rural	
C. Minerals	C. Communication	C. Wilderness	B. Summer work
D. Atmosphere	D. Advocacy	D. Laboratory	
E. Man-made	E. Care/maintenance	E. Advocacy group	C. Apprenticeships
goods	F. Recreation	F. Fund-raising organization	
F. Waste	G. Emergency services	G. Government agency	D. Entry-level work
management	H. Medical/health	H. Corporation	
G. Plants/trees	I. Conservation	I. Community group	E. Semiskilled and skilled work
H. Wildlife	J. Preservation	J. School/college	
I. Human	K. Restoration	K. Museum	F. Independent study
ecology	L. Recycling and	L. The "field"	
J. Energy	disposal		
	M. Agriculture		
	N. Aquaculture		
	O. Horticulture		

Energy Research Profile

Here's a summary of this profile: an apprenticeship in energy research at a laboratory, corporation, or government agency.

Two things have to be elaborated on initially in this profile: "energy" and, again, "research." This particular profile was done by one of my students, Harold, and we did the elaboration together. For "energy," he said he had in mind solar, wind, and biogas energy, as well as small-river-based and stream-based electricity generators. He had heard about the need for cheap nonpolluting power in underdeveloped countries and wanted to be able to help poor countries with their power needs. In fact, he said, that seemed a way for him to travel and be useful at the same time. He meant by "research" the invention and development of small, nonpolluting, inexpensive, energy-producing apparatuses, made for the most part with easily available resources.

Thus, his elaboration read:

> I want to apprentice at a place where there is research and development going on in the development of cheap, nonpolluting energy sources, that is, solar, biogas, wind, and water.

From here it was possible to get sources. Once he had articulated this, Harold said he was going to go to his favorite research library, an ecology center bookstore, and look up the names and addresses of energy organizations listed in books he was sure were there. He also decided to contact groups that did third-world development projects and ask them where he could learn useful skills so that he could join one of their programs in the future.

Profile
Forms 4 and 5:
WORK WITH ANIMALS
and
WORK WITH THINGS

WORK WITH ANIMALS

Focus of Work	Types of Work	Places of Work	Ways You Can Become Involved

A. Land animals
  1. free
  2. domesticated
  3. trained
  4. captive
B. Water animals
  1. free
  2. domestic
  3. trained
  4. captive
C. Birds
  1. free
  2. domestic
  3. trained
  4. captive
D. Insects
E. Reptiles
	A. Study of animals
	B. Preservation
	C. Conservation
	D. Restoration
	E. Advocacy
	F. Legal issues
	G. Training
	H. Breeding
	I. Farming
	J. Care
	K. Health/nutrition
	L. Competition
	M. Commerce
	N. Emergency rescue/disaster
	  management
	O. Education
	P. Control
	Q. Art/photography/film/
	  video
		A. Wilderness
		B. Urban
		C. Rural
		D. Laboratory
		E. Zoos
		F. Veterinary clinics, medical
		  facilities
		G. Kennels/boarding
		H. Training schools
		I. Pet shops
		J. Circuses
		K. Organizations and
		  advocacy groups
		L. Government
			A. Volunteer work
			
			B. Summer work
			
			C. Apprenticeships
			
			D. Entry-level work
			
			E. Semiskilled and skilled work
			
			F. Independent study

. . . .

WORK WITH THINGS
(BUILDING, INVENTING, AND EXPERIMENTING)

Focus of Work	Types of Work	Places of Work	Ways You Can Become Involved
A. Dwellings	A. Design	A. Laboratory	A. Volunteer work
B. Workplaces	B. Construction	B. Shop	
C. Recreation	C. Assembly	C. Office/studio	B. Summer work
facilities	D. Operation	D. Factory	
D. Toolmaking	E. Repair	E. Government	C. Apprenticeships
E. Vehicles	F. Reconstruction	F. Public organization	
F. Appliances	G. Creation/	G. Corporation	D. Entry-level work
G. Clothing	innovation	1. administration	
H. Toys/	H. Manufacture	2. work site	E. Semiskilled and skilled work
games	I. Sales	3. retail outlet	
I. Electronics	J. Advertising	4. sales office	F. Independent study
J. Computers	K. Fund-raising	H. Testing facility	
K. Communications	L. Regulation	I. Home	
L. Machines	M. Law and contracts	J. College/university	
M. Printing	N. Education		

HERE ARE two additional profiles, one dealing with WORK
WITH ANIMALS and the other with WORK WITH THINGS. The WORK
WITH ANIMALS profile form overlaps the ECOLOGICAL AND ENVI-
RONMENTAL WORK profile form a bit, but obviously emphasizes
the many distinct options for working with animals. You may be
surprised at the number of careers that are available in our society that involve working with animals.

If the category of working with animals seems a bit narrow,
working with things may seem too broad to fit into a single profile form. It encompasses building homes and office complexes,
making and using machines, developing and selling computers
and other electronic goods, designing toys and games, and manufacturing clothing. Each of these entries in the "Focus of
Work" column can be turned into a profile of its own in the
manner suggested in Chapter 26.

You should build your own forms if they seem appropriate
to your exploration of life's work. The detail in which you
examine any career choice has to do with the consequences of
exploring initial resources. Sometimes you have to begin all

over again if nothing works out, and you will find a new take on the same career can be helpful. Sometimes one gets enough information from a broad and general profile. There is no certain and single road to meaningful work, and the more flexible and patient you are, the more likely it is you'll find the right sources and the right place. The process is a bit like buying a house: There's lots of shopping around to do, many dead ends that may be encountered, and often you'll feel the temptation to give up on the quest and settle for something less than satisfactory. But selecting a life's work is an important act you have to live with, just as you have to live in the house you choose. In both cases patience is a powerful ally when you want to make the best decision. In addition, the very experience of gathering resources, observing many places of work, and going through many interviews will broaden your outlook, hone your discretionary powers, and in general stand you in good stead no matter what vocation you eventually choose. The quest is valuable experience in and of itself.

THE WORK WITH ANIMALS PROFILE FORM

It is surprising how many people in our society work with animals and how varied that work is. However, if you think of the number of pets people have, of the number of fish that swim in people's apartments, of the people who train guide dogs for the blind, use animals in medical and scientific experiments, or are involved in the protection of wildlife and wildlife environments, as well as farmworkers and the people who deal with animal health and safety, you get a picture of thousands of jobs in dozens of occupations. I have not seen any figures on the specific number of people who do animal-related work, but in the Yellow Pages of the San Francisco telephone book alone there are over fifty pet shops, over fifty pet supply stores, about one hundred veterinarians, and over twenty-five pet hospitals listed. In addition, in San Francisco, there are environmental groups dealing with the protection of wildlife, animal shelters and animal-control centers, a zoo, kennels, breeders, animal-boarding businesses, equestrian and canine obedience schools, and animal societies ranging all the way from the Humane Society and the Animal Liberation Front to pedigree dog and cat organizations, racing associations, and show horse groups. This, of course, doesn't even touch on the farm sector.

I know many youngsters who get a start working with animals doing everything from getting jobs on dairy farms (a very difficult thing to do—farm work is hard, pays low wages, and is often exploitative of "nonlegal" alien labor) to pet walking and volunteer work. Others get apprenticeships at veterinary clinics, animal space experiments for NASA conducted at a local university, and other animal experiments at local medical schools. In San Francisco there are kennels, zoos, and even two circuses. If a young person has an affinity for animals bordering on obsession it makes sense to take that preference seriously and help her or him meet people who have created careers out of working with animals. This could involve a trip to a school of veterinary medicine, a backstage visit to the zoo, or a tour of kennels and animal training schools. People who work with animals tend to be very willing to share their experiences and offer advice.

There are certain things to point out about this profile form before you use it. First, in the "Focus of Work" column, I have separated land animals, water animals, birds, insects, and reptiles even though work exists that involves more than one of these categories. If you want to work with all living creatures, just check all of the entries in the first column.

Second, under the land and water animal entries and the bird entry there are four separate subentries that refer to the different ways people relate to animals. There are free animals—that is, animals that live in their own environments and not under the control of people. This can refer to animals living in the wild, but it also relates to pigeons, rats, insects, and other life-forms that exist in rural communities and the cities alongside of (and sometimes chased by) people but not under their direct control.

. . . .

Then there are domesticated animals: animals bred or trained to be in the service of people. Some pets are domesticated, and food-producing animals are definitely domesticated. In addition to domesticated animals there are trained animals. Some horses are trained, some are domesticated but not highly trained, and some are free. The same is true with dogs and cats. The reason for the distinction between "domesticated" and "trained" is that different kinds of work are done with domesticated animals than with trained animals. Herding horses, for example, is not the same as training them.

Finally there are captive animals: fish in tanks, birds in cages, animals in zoos. Special considerations have to be made for captive animals and particular forms of work involved in caring for them.

I suppose I could have made the same distinctions for insects and reptiles, and if you want to add that refinement to the profile form please do if it helps focus on some particular career.

The rest of the profile form is pretty straightforward. A few comments, however, might be helpful. In the "Types of Work" column the entry "Study of animals" refers to research about the ways animals live in their natural environments and to laboratory experiments to learn about animal perception and behavior. It also refers to experiments on animals for human purposes, which is a very different matter. The study of animals for human purposes often involves deliberately infecting them with viruses and other disease carriers, eventually killing them and studying the corpses. There is a great deal of controversy over the use of animals for experimental purposes. It's important to be sensitive to these issues and clarify your own position when considering this avenue.

The entry "Care" refers to work that involves concern with the safety and health of animal environments. Organizations such as the ASPCA are concerned with animal welfare and try to counter cruelty, abandonment, and starvation of pets and other domesticated animals. Care can also be interpreted as "taking care of"— that is, baby-sitting and exercising animals.

A DESCRIPTION AND ANALYSIS OF THE PROFILES

. . . .

The entry "Control" refers to controlling ill or rabid animals or those that have gone wild and are threats to people, other animals, and themselves. Usually this is done through county or local departments. For some tasks the work requires a great deal of nerve and skill.

Finally, the entry "Art/photography/film/video" refers to people in the media who specialize in the documentation of animal life. This work ranges from documenting the daily lives of animals in their natural environments on film to magazine, calendar, and poster photography.

The last two columns are self-explanatory.

Here are two WORK WITH ANIMALS profiles for you to elaborate upon if you are interested in working with animals. Even if your own profile, when completed, is quite different, brainstorming with these two profiles may help you generate some novel ideas and leads you'll be able to use.

WORK WITH ANIMALS

Focus of Work	Types of Work	Places of Work	Ways You Can Become Involved
A. Land animals 　1. free 　2. domesticated 　3. trained 　4. captive B. Water animals 　1. free 　2. domestic 　3. trained 　4. captive C. Birds 　1. free 　2. domestic 　3. trained 　4. captive D. Insects E. Reptiles	A. Study of animals B. Preservation C. Conservation D. Restoration E. Advocacy F. Legal issues G. Training H. Breeding I. Farming J. Care K. Health/nutrition L. Competition M. Commerce N. Emergency rescue/disaster 　management O. Education P. Control Q. Art/photography/film/ 　video	A. Wilderness B. Urban C. Rural D. Laboratory E. Zoos F. Veterinary clinics, medical 　facilities G. Kennels/boarding H. Training schools I. Pet shops J. Circuses K. Organizations and 　advocacy groups L. Government	A. Volunteer work B. Summer work C. Apprenticeships D. Entry-level work E. Semiskilled and skilled work F. Independent study

Sample Profile # 1

.

. . . .

WORK WITH ANIMALS

Focus of Work	Types of Work	Places of Work	Ways You Can Become Involved
A. Land animals	A. Study of animals	A. Wilderness	A. Volunteer work
1. free	B. Preservation	B. Urban	
2. domesticated	C. Conservation	C. Rural	B. Summer work
3. trained	D. Restoration	D. Laboratory	
4. captive	E. Advocacy	E. Zoos	C. Apprenticeships
B. Water animals	F. Legal issues	F. Veterinary clinics, medical	
1. free	G. Training	facilities	D. Entry-level work
2. domestic	H. Breeding	G. Kennels/boarding	
3. trained	I. Farming	H. Training schools	E. Semiskilled and skilled work
4. captive	J. Care	I. Pet shops	
C. Birds	K. Health/nutrition	J. Circuses	F. Independent study
1. free	L. Competition	K. Organizations and	
2. domestic	M. Commerce	advocacy groups	
3. trained	N. Emergency rescue/disaster	L. Government	
4. captive	management		
D. Insects	O. Education		
E. Reptiles	P. Control		
	Q. Art/photography/film/		
	video		

Sample Profile #2

THE WORK WITH THINGS PROFILE FORM

The WORK WITH THINGS profile form is an attempt to encapsulate into one profile form many different kinds of activity that have as their common feature working directly with or on the development of man-made objects. Going down the "Focus of Work" column, the first three entries describe facilities such as:

A. Dwelling places—that is, homes, apartment houses, tents, houseboats, and so forth

B. Workplaces—such as factories, shops, garages, offices, and studios

C. Recreation facilities—such as stadiums, swimming pools, ski lifts, and parks

The entry "Toolmaking" refers to the development and fashioning of tools and instruments ranging from telescopes and electron microscopes to lathes, grinding machines, shovels, and hammers. The toolmaking industry is one of the most essential ones in our economy. Many different kinds of tools are needed, and the invention of new tools can lead to major developments in science and technology. Information about toolmaking can be obtained from the Machinists Union and from scientific instrument makers, computer corporations, and engineering organizations. Toolmaking involves skills such as lens grinding, die cutting, electronic and mechanical design, and model making.

The entry "Vehicles" refers to any man-made objects that move people and things. This ranges from skateboards to jet planes.

The entry "Appliances" also has a wide range, encompassing mainly household items such as toasters, stoves, washing machines, and more.

The entry "Machines" is also somewhat ambiguous. It refers to engines, derricks, pumps, conveyer belts, and all of the other machinery used in manufacture. If you choose this entry, be sure to elaborate on what machines or categories of machines you mean.

The other entries in the profile form should be self-evident. If you have any questions, refer back to the WORK WITH PEOPLE and the WORK IN MEDIA AND THE ARTS profile forms, which explain them in some detail.

Here are two sample WORK WITH THINGS profiles, along with some comments on who did them and how they worked out.

Joanna

Here's a summary of this profile: volunteer or apprentice work in computers focused on creation, innovation, repair, and reconstruction, in a shop setting.

Joanna, who filled out this profile, explained that she had been hanging around arcades, computer stores, and hackers' groups since she was twelve. She wanted to get involved in the computer world, learn about sophisticated programming as well as electronics, and find a way to support herself. She indi-

WORK WITH THINGS
(BUILDING, INVENTING, AND EXPERIMENTING)

Focus of Work	Types of Work	Places of Work	Ways You Can Become Involved
A. Dwellings	A. Design	A. Laboratory	A. Volunteer work
B. Workplaces	B. Construction	B. Shop	
C. Recreation	C. Assembly	C. Office/studio	B. Summer work
facilities	D. Operation	D. Factory	
D. Toolmaking	E. Repair	E. Government	C. Apprenticeships
E. Vehicles	F. Reconstruction	F. Public organization	
F. Appliances	G. Creation/	G. Corporation	D. Entry-level work
G. Clothing	Innovation	1. administration	
H. Toys/	H. Manufacture	2. work site	E. Semiskilled and skilled work
games	I. Sales	3. retail outlet	
I. Electronics	J. Advertising	4. sales office	F. Independent study
J. Computers	K. Fund-raising	H. Testing facility	
K. Communications	L. Regulation	I. Home	
L. Machines	M. Law and contracts	J. College/university	
M. Printing	N. Education		

Joanna's Profile

cated that filling out the profile was for her a focusing act, a useful way of summarizing her current situation and developing a plan for the next few years.

Joanna had never felt comfortable in formal educational settings and didn't want to go to college. She didn't drop out of high school; she just, as she put it, faded away without anyone at the school noticing or caring. Her current idea was to develop new artistic uses for home computers and to find ways to take machines that were no longer in production and, through cannibalizing them and recombining the parts, create new machines that would be moderately powerful. She also wanted to help people who had been fooled into buying computers that had no service backups. She figured that repairing, rebuilding, and creating new uses for computers should be challenging and provide a way for her to make a modest living. She decided, after writing out her elaboration on the profile, that her best resources would be computer shops, hackers' and owners' groups, and some of the free software exchanges she participated in. After a few weeks she found a small computer repair shop run by two people who had worked in the research division at Atari and who combined their own development work with repairing computers that had no backup repair services. They took her on as a nonpaid apprentice for a trial period of a month, and will begin to pay her if things work out after that time.

Franklin

WORK WITH THINGS
(BUILDING, INVENTING, AND EXPERIMENTING)

Focus of Work	Types of Work	Places of Work	Ways You Can Become Involved
A. Dwellings	A. Design	A. Laboratory	A. Volunteer work
B. Workplaces	B. Construction	B. Shop	
C. Recreation	C. Assembly	C. Office/studio	B. Summer work
facilities	D. Operation	D. Factory	
D. Toolmaking	E. Repair	E. Government	C. Apprenticeships
E. Vehicles	F. Reconstruction	F. Public organization	
F. Appliances	G. Creation/	G. Corporation	D. Entry-level work
G. Clothing	innovation	1. administration	
H. Toys/	H. Manufacture	2. work site	E. Semiskilled and skilled work
games	I. Sales	3. retail outlet	
I. Electronics	J. Advertising	4. sales office	F. Independent study
J. Computers	K. Fund-raising	H. Testing facility	
K. Communications	L. Regulation	I. Home	
L. Machines	M. Law and contracts	J. College/university	
M. Printing	N. Education		

Franklin's Profile

Here's a summary of this profile: apprenticeship work with the design and construction of machines in a shop or factory.

Franklin did this elaboration with his father and summarized what they came up with in this way:

I want to work with steel and other metals that go into the making of machines. For years my hobby has been to build metal models of derricks, cranes, and bridges, and to invent elaborate systems of gears and pulleys that lifted and poured and pushed earth and water. I would like to spend a year or two working in a factory where large-scale construction machines are put together, as well as work with people who design these and other kinds of machines. The first thing to do is visit factories and also go to the design and engineering departments of City College and find a way to meet people involved in design. It may be possible that engineering school will be the right choice for me in a few years, but I would like to get a feel for the work before commiting myself to four or five years of study.

· · · · · · · · · · · · · · · · · · · *26* ·

A
Do-It-Yourself
Work Profile Form
and
Some Exercises
in Profile Making

THE PROFILES elaborated on in this book were chosen to cover the widest range of interesting work that could reasonably be encompassed in a single book. They focus on work with people, the environment, animals, and things, as well as work in media and the arts. I picked these areas because they are perhaps the historically oldest forms of human work and have been elaborated on throughout the centuries. Nevertheless, it is not possible to be exhaustive about them, much less incorporate many of the other forms of work people do. The profile form I adopted for presentation of work choices in the book does, however, provide a way for you to develop your own profiles for other areas of work as well as to elaborate further on the profiles I've come up with. A blank profile form follows, with some examples and suggestions on how you can go about profile building.

The blank form on page 246 might be called a Do-It-Yourself Work Profile Form.

The blank profile form can be used in several ways to generate new work profiles:

1. As an exercise in the development of new profiles that analyze careers not covered in this book.

Many jobs that people do aren't covered here. It would probably take an encyclopedia to encompass all of productive human activity, but open-ended profiles and ingenuity can help you zero in on and analyze work in any area you come up with.

Pick some kind of work not already worked into a profile, such as communications, health, or athletics, and make up your own profile form. This will get you thinking about the variety of ways in which one can define work related to a specific type of human activity. On page 247 is a start for one on athletics. Try to complete it and go on in the area of health or communications yourself. For parents, this practice can serve the additional purpose of fine-tuning your skills as a career counselor, making it easy to share advice about post–high school careers with other adults who have children in high school.

2. As an elaboration on one of the profiles in the book.

For example, if you decide to focus on the "Toys/games" entry in the WORK WITH THINGS profile form, a WORK WITH TOYS AND GAMES subprofile form can be created to fine-tune your exploration of that field. It might look something like the one on page 248.

A DO-IT-YOURSELF WORK PROFILE FORM

Focus of Work	Types of Work	Places of Work	Ways You Can Become Involved
A.	A.	A.	A. Volunteer work
B.	B.	B.	B. Summer work
C.	C.	C.	
D.	D.	D.	C. Apprenticeships
E.	E.	E.	
F.	F.	F.	D. Entry-level work
G.	G.	G.	
H.	H.	H.	E. Semiskilled and skilled work
I.	I.	I.	
J.	J.	J.	F. Independent study
K.	K.	K.	
L.	L.	L.	
M.	M.	M.	
N.	N.	N.	

WORK IN ATHLETICS

Focus of Work	Types of Work	Places of Work	Ways You Can Become Involved
A. Exercise/health	A. Competition	A. Competition	A. Volunteer work
B. Coaching	B. Arts	B. Shop	
C. Equipment	C. Design	C. Office/studio	B. Summer work
D. Safety	D. Publicity	D. School	
E. Refereeing	E. Sales/financing	E. Community center	C. Apprenticeships
F. Facilities	F. Teaching	F. Organization	
G.	G.	G.	D. Entry-level work
H.	H.	H.	
I.	I.	I.	E. Semiskilled and skilled work
J.	J.	J.	
K.			F. Independent study
L.			
M.			

WORK WITH TOYS AND GAMES

Focus of Work	Types of Work	Places of Work	Ways You Can Become Involved
A. Strategy	A. Design	A. Competition	A. Volunteer work
B. Electronics	B. Construction	B. Shop	B. Summer work
C. Learning	C. Assembly	C. Office/studio	C. Apprenticeships
D. Child development	D. Operation	D. School	D. Entry-level work
E. Fantasy and conflict	E. Repair	E. Community center	E. Semiskilled and skilled work
F. Paper and pencil	F. Reconstruction	F. Organization	F. Independent study
G. Magic	G. Creation/innovation	G. Corporation	
H. Mechanical	H. Manufacture	1. administration	
I. Construction	I. Sales	2. work site	
J. Dolls and action figures	J. Advertising	3. retail outlet	
K. Models	K. Fund-raising	4. sales office	
L. Chance and gambling games	L. Regulation	H. Testing facility	
	M. Law and contracts	I. Home	
	N. Education	J. College/university	

part four

. . . .

Common Questions from Anxious Parents

CHAPTER

27

. . . And
Some
Reassuring
Responses

CERTAIN QUESTIONS frequently arise in discussions I've had with parents about what might happen to youngsters who don't go straight to college after high school. Here are eight of the most common questions they ask me, as well as some answers that may alleviate some of the anxiety parents feel when their children do something out of the ordinary.

Question 1: *Will my child be penalized if she or he tries to get into college the next year instead of right after graduation?*
In order to answer this, I called the undergraduate admissions offices of twenty colleges that represented a cross section

of public and private institutions. The admissions officers were very generous with their time, and I advise you to do what I did yourself if you have any questions about how a particular college deals with delayed applications.

The first thing that all of the admissions officers said is that one of the greatest problems with delayed admissions is getting student dossiers completed and sent in from high schools after students have been out of school for a while. They said that teachers move, administrators change, filing systems are revised or purged. The solution, one that is crucial, is to *have a completed dossier, including grades, SAT scores, and recommendations, as well as a student essay, completed before graduation whether or not your child goes to college after high school.* Also, be sure you know who is responsible for preserving that dossier, and if at all possible get a copy yourself. One way to do this is to have confidential references sealed by the school and sent to you by registered mail, so that any authority can tell whether you've opened them or not. Some schools will do this, others won't. In any case, know who has your child's dossier.

In order to know what goes in the dossier, send away for a state college or university application, and for several private college applications, and have your child fill them out as if she or he were applying. Also get a record of SAT scores and an official copy of your child's grade transcript. The recommendations are essential; be sure they are done and sealed if you can't get copies. Make sure your child's college folder is complete before she or he graduates from high school.

I failed to do this for my oldest daughter, and her application to college, which was submitted the year after she graduated high school, almost didn't make it to the college on time. We had to assemble it piece by piece, and her application was given low priority by the high school, which was working on the applications of current graduates. We made sure for our other children that their applications were complete as soon as possible.

There's another hint that might be useful if your child applies to college the year after high school. Many colleges have what is called early admission. Early admission is designed for students who have one first-choice college that they will attend, if accepted, no matter where else they may be accepted. You can only apply for early admission to one college, and all of the other colleges you apply to will know that you have applied for early admission somewhere. Your chances of getting into the college of your choice are increased by applying for early admission. You hear from that college earlier than usual (sometimes as early as January 1), and if you are accepted your applications are pulled from all of the other colleges you applied to.

As for the status of delayed applications: Every college I spoke to accepts delayed applications without prejudice. Some private institutions, such as Harvard and Columbia, suggest that students contemplating delayed admission still apply in their senior year of high school; they give automatic delayed attendance to any student who is accepted and requests a year off. They will hold a place for the next year and reapplication is not necessary. On the other hand, they said that it was perfectly all right to apply a year or two after graduation also. However, *all of the colleges I contacted said that delayed applications should be accompanied by an essay description of what was done during the year after high school.* Heavy emphasis is placed upon educational or interesting work and travel experiences during that year. In fact, the admissions officer at the University of California, Berkeley, told me that an interesting year between high school and college gives an application "brownie points," and jobs like working for the Forestry Service or teaching English at a Berlitz school in Thailand increase the chance for admission.

Working for money to attend college is usually considered a valid reason to delay application. However, schools such as Harvard have grants based on need and suggest that, if money is the only need, a student should still apply; if she or he is accepted, the college will provide the funds and a work-study job if necessary.

State colleges and universities, unlike private institutions, do not hold places for delayed entrance. They suggest that you apply the year you want to attend and include an account of the years between high school and college with the application. The admissions officers of state schools told me they look very favorably on older students because they tend to be more serious and have a lower dropout level.

Question 2: *What if my child did very badly in high school, has an educationally rich and motivating year after high school, and then decides to go to a good college? How can several bad years in high school be negated?*

Several things can be done to wipe out a disastrous high school career. First of all, six months of reliable work indicates a dedication that may not have existed during high school. Consequently, college recommendations from people at work become very important, and can negate bad or indifferent recommendations from high school. This is particularly true if the work is interesting and involves some form of creative or intellectual activity, and makes serious demands on the worker. Other nonschool recommendations from people with status in your community are also very useful. Choose these very carefully. Build a new case for admission altogether.

In addition, it is possible to retake the SATs the year after high school, and if one does significantly better than when in high school, the new scores can usually replace the old ones.

Another thing that will impress admissions officers is grades on correspondence courses or in junior college courses. This is particularly true if the courses resemble freshman humanities, writing, or social sciences courses; are in the sciences; or are directly related to the work one is doing.

Essentially what you want to do is build up a convincing case that, even though high school was not a positive experience, the year after high school was a time of maturing, and college is now a meaningful option that can be handled with ease.

Question 3: *What happens if, after a year of trying out a certain area of work, my child changes his mind and decides it's not for*

him? Will that be a wasted year and give him the habit of flit-
ting from one thing to another without making any serious
commitments?

People who feel an affinity for a certain vocation and work
at it for a year are likely to discover a great deal about themselves. The very process of getting out of a formal school setting
and working to acquire a vocation instead of merely to make
money is itself a model of what life might be like. Some people
will certainly flit from one thing to another, whether they go to
college or not. Others will try a few things until they discover
what is right for them. The process, whether it works the first
time or not, is valuable as an act of self-definition. My experience has been that, whether or not they continued on the path
they initially set out for themselves, young people who have
tried to find their own paths have become more confident about
their ability, ultimately, to find the right place for themselves.
They are not afraid of work and of taking the initiative rather
than waiting for opportunities to come to them.

It is rare that work the year after high school becomes a
paralyzing, negative experience. If it seems to be going that
way, it is very important to support your child and encourage
her to broaden her exploration and find another place for herself. However, it's equally important to be sensitive to the fact
that new routines have their petty frustrations, and learning
new things can be difficult as well as rewarding. Don't jump in
too fast to suggest your children change direction, and at the
same time don't get in their way if they see no other option.
Just be there for them and think of how long (if at all) it took
you to settle into comfortable, rewarding work.

Question 4: *What if we come up with a complete dead end in*
the search for a particular placement?

There will be times when you can't find a placement in the
area of work that you want. This is particularly true for people
who live in rural areas or small towns. For example, where I
live there is no industry or university, and very little by way of
creative work. Most high school graduates who do not go on to
college and want to do more than work in a shop or in the tour-

ist or logging and fishing industries have to move to the nearest small city (population 120,000) to find work, apprenticeships, and training. There are several things one can do if the original search for a placement comes to a dead end:

1. Find a way to help your child redefine his choice and approximate his ideal situation as closely as possible. For example, if he wants to do metal sculpture and live in a rural area, the closest he might be able to come to that choice is to get an apprenticeship with someone who shoes horses. Usually farriers, in addition to shoeing horses, do wrought iron work and sometimes work with other metals as well. Combining apprenticeship with a farrier with some correspondence courses in sculpture and art history might provide useful skills and knowledge and give him a forge to work at to produce his own sculpture. In addition, visits to galleries and studios in the nearest city can fill out a productive year.

This may not work out, of course; other options might be to work with clay or wood for a while, or find someone who does soldering or has a metal forge and creates small pieces of sculpture or sculptured jewelry.

Take another example: Suppose your child wants to do TV news and sports, and there is no TV studio or station in your town. There are some things she can do if she can get the use of a video camera. She might set herself up as a local video artist and videotape weddings and birthday parties, as well as community and athletic events. In order to develop skills she can enroll in a video correspondence class and spend several weekends going to a city where there is a university or college extension program that holds weekend classes. If she can't find specific classes in TV video, look through the college's catalog and see whether there are classes in video for teachers or for anthropologists or any other professional. Often good classes in the arts are tucked away into other departments. After spending several months setting herself up and doing videos, she might take the best of her work and begin to explore options in TV in a big city nearby. Her own work and experience will provide her with a portfolio. If she wants to look fancy, she might even print up a business card. Thus she can combine work in your own community with college classes and weekend workshops, and after six months begin to reach out and find out how to continue on a larger scale if she wants.

The important thing to realize is that it takes a bit of creativity and a lot of persistence to mold the world and yourself a bit to fit your needs. With patience and ingenuity, however, the most unlikely things become possible.

2. Move to a larger place. If your child has friends working or attending college in some nearby city, he could see if he could move in and share the rent with them temporarily. He can get a part-time job, a McDonald's special, to give himself time to look around and find a placement. Many young people I've worked with have done this and found that after a month or two they can find apprenticeships, volunteer work, and occasionally jobs in everything ranging from theater to medical, legal, and architectural offices, and from ecology organizations to nursing homes.

It's sensible, if one chooses the option of moving to another place, to spend several weeks or even months searching for the *right* place and placement rather than committing to a strange situation blindly.

Question 5: *Is it sensible for parents to initiate the idea of exploring some form of vocation the year after high school if they observe that their child wants to spend the year after high school partying, in or out of college?*

My answer is: Yes, but be careful. It is very easy to bruise adolescent sensibility and create conflict even though you mean well. Some teenagers' initial response to any suggestion about what to do with their lives will range from "Will you leave me alone" to "It's none of your business." There are a number of ways to bring up the subject, none of them guaranteed to work, but all of which provide a face-saving way out for you and your children. One is to give them a copy of this book and suggest they read it. If they don't, there's nothing lost; don't make a big deal out of it.

You can also tell them you've been reading the book, and show them the profile forms and suggest that they look through them or that you look through them together. The crucial thing is to bring up the issue of options for the year after high school late in the junior year of high school or early in the senior year. Don't wait until the last minute. Perhaps the ideal situation would be to bring up the option of exploring potentially rewarding work at the same time the issue of choosing a college is first discussed. The work option can seem less onerous in the context of being one of a number of options available after high school. That way, there also will be time for your daughter or son to look at the profile forms as well as college catalogs and have adequate time to weigh and measure what to do.

If you *are* down to the last minute, a sensible strategy might be to order correspondence college catalogs as well as undergraduate catalogs and provide them to your children along with this or some other book that suggests work options.

Be explicit about your feelings about the necessity of going to college right after high school, and if you are not sure what the best option is, make that clear. Your uncertainty can provide a nonthreatening context in which options can be discussed without making your child feel that her or his life is being planned by someone else.

Question 6: *What should we do with the money we saved for our children's college education if they decide not to go straight to college?*

Whatever your children decide, I do not think that money that has been saved for education should ever be shifted into a general fund and lose its designated purpose. That money, no matter how modest or great, is an investment in your children's future and should be considered untouchable except in the most extreme circumstances.

However, I suggest that money saved for college be thought of in a broader context, as money saved for educational purposes. All education does not necessarily take place at college. There are some paying apprenticeships, private or group teaching arrangements (as in music, theater, the arts, and many skilled crafts), and educational travel experiences (such as archaeological or marine biological voyages) that are as important as college. There are times when educational money may have to be used for equipment costs, or for membership fees in organizations. It's a matter of using what money you have sensibly and being sure that your children are not just functioning on the basis of a whim. In my experience, one way to tell this is whether your children are willing to work and share educational expenses with you.

It is also important, for the sake of clarity and honesty in the family, for your children to know how much money you have put aside for education, as well as the limits on the ways in which it can be spent.

As a final comment here, if your children don't need educational money the year after high school, keep the money in the bank, let it accrue interest, and use it later—since education, at its best, is a lifelong activity.

Question 7: *Can't this book be used by youngsters already in college, or by adults who are thinking of changing careers in midlife, or looking for new work to do after retirement?*
The ideas in this book apply to the relationship of personal fulfillment to work at any age. If you feel that the work you do is less meaningful than it could or should be, or boring, and that you spend your working hours waiting for "real time" when you do things that give you pleasure and make you feel of use to others, then you face the same choices and the same possibilities as someone coming out of high school who is about to embark on the quest for meaningful life's work. The psychological and economical conditions of your life might be different than those of younger people, your experience broader and your obligations greater, but the need to learn new, meaningful ways of functioning is no different. In fact, it is even possible to pursue your own affinities for life's work with your son or

daughter, for your sake as well as for theirs. They might help you gather the courage to be who you wish you could be, and will themselves certainly appreciate the opportunity you have given them to help you.

My children have helped me through some difficult times in my life, and I learned about their love for me through that help. I also saw how they appreciated the moment to return the love they had received. Children need opportunities to be of use to their parents and show them support and provide them with advice. Mutual assistance is one of the great lasting bonds in family life, and when it does not exist, resentment can easily develop.

Learn for yourself, with your children, and share their learning when possible. The quest for meaningful work, at any stage in life, can be a family matter, each person on her or his own adventure with the support and advice of all of the others.

Question 8: *Can my children make a living doing what they want to do? Isn't there some danger in being so romantic when the next generation will eventually have to settle down, have a family, buy a house, and send their own children to expensive colleges?*

The kinds of work described in this book are open-ended and can lead, eventually, to decently paid, personally rewarding careers. The book is not about how to become a millionaire, or how to retire at twenty-eight, or how to parlay one hundred dollars into one million dollars over ten years. It is for people who value the quality of their lives more than the quantity of what they own and can buy. It tries to introduce young people to careers that will develop their talents and give them rewards so that life and work are integrated harmoniously. It also tries to help them become active and take control of their work lives, rather than go where the money is or settle for whatever is available.

Most of the work described here can lead to a decent middle-class or upper-middle-class life, a modest but full life that leaves time to grow personally and help others.

. . . .

Certainly most people who try this road to work will eventually settle down, have families, and worry about the future. So will other people whose jobs do not provide a stable center or inner satisfaction. There is no guarantee, in our society, of stability in work or economic security. All the more reason, then, to develop the confidence to live modestly and build lives based on rewarding work, sustaining personal relationships, and social generosity. Then the question of settling down and raising a family does not have to lead to the sacrifice of self and social commitment. In a shared, decent life everyone pulls together and problems become family problems for all to help solve. That doesn't guarantee an easy life, but what does in our society, where people often have to fend for themselves without familial or social support? It may indeed be better to have islands of sustaining strength in one's life than to rush headlong into a life of competition if one hopes to survive and even thrive in our society at the end of this century.

Appendix

. . . .

Resources and References for the Investigation of Life's Work

Personal Request Letter

Many books and pamphlets provide useful leads for the exploration of the career choices generated by the profile forms in this book. Many are readily available in public libraries. Others can be obtained from the U.S. Government Printing Office, which has outlets in most major cities, or in bookstores, or directly from publishers. There are also dozens of professional and volunteer organizations that provide career information and suggestions about people to contact for information and even jobs.

It's useful to prepare a personalized request letter to send to organizations and publishers. Also, whenever possible, try to discover the name of an individual who is responsible for providing the information you want and send your request to that person. *Always make your quest for information, contacts, and interviews personal.*

Always include the following in your personal request letter:

1. A brief description of your career interests and your current school or work status
2. A clear statement of what you want to order
3. A request for any additional information that might be relevant, as well as the phone numbers and addresses of other resources to contact
4. A thank-you

It also helps to enclose a stamped, self-addressed 8½-by-11 envelope. To find out the right amount of postage to include, put any thirty-two-page pamphlet in the envelope and have it weighed for postage at the post office.

Here's a sample personal request letter (notice the format, a very common one for request letters).

> September 20, 1990
> 10 Ridge Drive
> Cococino, CA 44226

Director
Summer Work Program
Smithsonian Institution
Office of Oceanography and Limnology
Washington, D.C. 20560

Dear Director,

I am currently a senior at Cococino High School. Over the past few years I have become interested in exploring a career in oceanography, and have taken several correspondence courses in the subject. I have also worked during the past few summers at the local dock unloading, cleaning, and packing fish. Our community borders on the Pacific Ocean and I've grown up interested in studying and preserving the ocean environment.

Recently I heard that you provide a number of summer jobs or apprenticeships in oceanography. I would appreciate it if you could send me information about this work as well as any applications that you have available.

Enclosed is a self-addressed stamped envelope.

If you have any additional information about whom to contact about jobs or apprenticeships in oceanography I would appreciate hearing about them.

Thank you for your kind attention to my letter.

Sincerely,

Karl Katz

Government Resources

1. The U.S. Department of Labor's Employment and Training Administration publishes a *Dictionary of Occupational Titles* that is updated every few years. The dictionary is over 1,300 pages long and contains all of the job designations used by the government when it studies the economy. The jobs are organized by occupational category and are broken down into groups and subgroups. Each particular job is then briefly described. In addition, supplements to the dictionary are published annually.

Most libraries have copies of the dictionary, which is also available from the U.S. Government Printing Office. Though I don't think it's worth buying one, it makes sense to peruse it at the library, because it is a good source of specific job definitions in almost any imaginable area of work.

2. The U.S. Department of Labor's Bureau of Labor Statistics publishes an annual book about 500 pages long titled the *Occupational Outlook Handbook.* The handbook contains

descriptions of hundreds of job categories. For each category there is a brief description of the nature of the work, working conditions, the number of people employed in that work, the training and qualifications for the job, the job outlook and earnings, a description of related occupations, and a list of sources of additional information. This book is extremely valuable and it's worth investing the twenty-three dollars it costs to have the information it provides immediately available. Of course, you could also use a library copy.

3. For information about temporary summer jobs with the federal government, write:

> Summer Employment, GPA Desk
> U.S. Civil Service Desk
> 1900 E St. NW
> Washington, DC 20415

Ask for Announcement 414 and write as early in the school year as possible. Remember that in order to get federal employment you must fill out Federal Employment Form 57, which you can also get from the Civil Service Commission and from many post offices.

4. Another source for interesting summer employment is the National Science Foundation (1800 G St., Washington, DC 20550). It publishes a series of free booklets on the jobs it offers and they are worth writing for.

5. If you are interested in a career in the civil service of the federal government, it also makes sense to take a look at a copy of ARCO Publishing's *Civil Service Handbook: How to Get a Civil Service Job.*

6. Other government agencies to write for job information are:

- the field and regional offices of the Bureau of Apprenticeship, the U.S. Department of Labor (listed in the phone book under "U.S. Government Offices." If there is none in your location, ask federal information for the nearest office.)

- state apprenticeship agencies listed under each state's department of labor

General Resources

Here are a number of library reference books that provide useful information about organizations that deal with vocation and counseling:

- *Directory of Counseling Services,* published by the American Association for Counseling and Development (5999 Stevenson Avenue, Alexandria, VA 22304), provides information on vocational and many other types of counseling.
- *Encyclopedia of Careers and Vocational Guidance* (J. G. Ferguson Co., distributed by Doubleday).
- *The Guide to American Directories, The Dictionary of Directories,* and the *Encyclopedia of Associations* all provide names and addresses of organizations, associations, businesses, and individuals throughout the country. Most libraries have copies and these can be used to search for specific contacts even in the most specialized fields.

Correspondence and Home Learning Classes

1. The National Home Study Association provides information about home study programs. They are located at 1601 18th St. NW, Washington, DC 20009 (phone: 202-234-5100). Among their many publications is *Directory of Accredited Home Study Schools.*

2. A directory of university-based correspondence courses entitled *Guide to Independent Study Through Correspondence* is published by the National University Extension Association and is available from Peterson's Guides, Box 2123, Princeton, NJ 08540. The directory is organized by study areas and gives a list of universities that provide classes in those areas. For example, you would find listings under such subjects as agriculture, engineering, music, and education, each of which would have many subheadings and lists of schools that provide classes in those subheadings. High school students and graduates qualify to take most of those classes without having any college experience, and many of them provide college transfer credit.

Career and Vocational Guidance Series

A number of publishing houses have series of books on careers and vocations. These books provide introductions to specific careers and give lists and resources. Most libraries and large bookstores carry one or more of the series. I've looked through dozens of these books and find them all easy reading and most valuable for the references they provide. They are good library or bookstore reading. Probably the most likely place to find a collection of these books is in the vocations section of your local high school's library or in the office of the high school counselor. Here are a few of the most popular series with a sampling of the titles they offer:

1. ARCO Career Guidance Series (available from ARCO, 219 Park Avenue South, New York, NY 10003). Some of their titles are:

- *Your Future in Animal Services*
- *Your Future in Art and Design*
- *Your Future in Broadcasting*

Other titles deal with broadcasting, electronics and computers, forestry, medical technology, photography, technical and science writing, and so on.

2. The Vocational Education Series, published by Vocational Guidance Manuals (235 East 45 St., New York, NY 10017), includes titles on careers such as acting, dancing, foreign service, free-lance writing, geology, machine shop trades, oceanographic careers, printing, textiles, and so on.

3. The Julian Messner Company in New York publishes many vocational titles such as *Crafts: A Career Alternative*, by

Carol S. Kushner, and *Careers to Preserve Our Shrinking World: Living and Working with Appropriate Technology,* by Robert V. Doyle.

Additional References and Resources

1. *The World Almanac* and *The Information Please Almanac,* which are updated every year, have lists of organizations and associations that include thousands of entries. These groups include professional and student associations, environmental groups, and many other types of organizations, many of which provide career information. These lists are the most up-to-date you can find and are worth the price of the books. The almanacs also provide information about jobs and careers, plus many other facts, figures, names, and addresses that might turn out to be useful.

2. *Getting Work Experience: The College Student's Directory of Summer Internship Programs That Lead to Careers,* by Betsy Bauer (New York: Dell, 1985), lists dozens of internship programs in the arts, business, the sciences, media, government, and other fields, and the book gives detailed information on how to make contacts. Even though most of the internships described in the book seem to be for college students, I think sincere and experienced high school graduates might be considered if they write interesting letters of introduction and convince interviewers that they are sincere about considering following up the internship with a career.

3. There are a number of resources for student travel, socially responsible domestic and international work, and educational exchanges. One interesting pamphlet is *Alternatives to the Peace Corps: Gaining Third World Experience,* by Becky Buell and Karl Hamerschlag (published by and available from the Institute for Food and Development Policy, 145 Ninth St., San Francisco, CA 94303; phone: 415-864-8555). This lists many exchange programs that provide young people with experiences working on development projects in the underdeveloped world. Most of the projects mentioned have church sponsorship and are quite reliable and responsible. However, if you decide to become involved in a program it makes sense to learn about its history, the qualifications of the staff, and the resources it has at its command. If possible, it also makes sense to talk to people who have been through the program. Here are two umbrella organizations listed in the book that you might contact:

> Interaction (American Council for Voluntary International Action)
> 200 Park Avenue South, New York, NY 10003
> Phone: 212-777-8210
>
> CODEL (Coordination in Development)
> 475 Riverside Drive
> New York, NY 10115
> Phone: 212-870-3000

Another organization that brings young people from all over the country together to consider issues of community participation and social responsibility is:

> The Encampment for Citizenship
> 717 61st Street
> Oakland, CA 94609
> Phone: 415-420-5777

This organization is connected with many community projects and conducts summer sessions throughout the country. It is more than fifty years old and has a fine reputation.

Other organizations that arrange for work and study exchanges are:

> Center for Interim Programs
> 233 Mount Lucas Road
> Princeton, NJ 08540
> Phone: 609-924-0441
>
> Earthwatch Expeditions
> 680 Mount Auburn Street
> Watertown, MA 02272

In addition, here are a number of catalogs, journals, and contacts that provide leads for socially responsible internships and voluntary programs:

International Directory for Youth Internships
Learning Resources in International Studies
777 United Nations Plaza
New York, NY 10017

Environmental Opportunities
EOV
P.O. Box 969
Stowe, VT 05672

Overseas List
Opportunities for Living and Working in Developing
    Countries
Augsburg Publishing House
Minneapolis, MN 55415

International Workcamp Directory
VFP International Workcamps
Tiffany Road
Belmont, NY 11201

*Work, Study, Travel Abroad: The Whole World Hand-
    book*, by Marjorie A. Cohen
        and
Student Travel Catalog
Council on International Educational Exchange
205 East 42 Street
New York, NY 10017

Community Jobs
Box 1205N
1516 P St. NW
Washington, DC 20005

Helping Out in the Outdoors
American Hiking Society
1015 31st Street
Washington, DC 20007.

The Student Conservation Association
P.O. Box 550
Charlestown, NH 03603

Youth Conservation Corps
Director
Division of Manpower Training and Youth Conserva-
tion Programs
United States Forest Service
U.S. Department of Agriculture
Washington, DC 20250

4. Finally, here are a number of miscellaneous
resources that might be of use in the quest for information
about certain forms of work. I keep a notebook to record
sources like these that have no immediate use but might be
of interest to some youngsters in the future. It makes sense
to keep a list of potential resources that might be of use to
your children and their friends. Many of them can be found
in the educational ad sections of magazines, newspapers,
and professional journals.

Archaeological Fieldwork Opportunities Bulletin
Archaeological Institute of America
675 Commonwealth Avenue
Boston, MA 02215

Raptor Centers for the Care of Birds Damaged in the
Wild or by Natural or Human Caused Disasters:

- Carolina Raptor Center
  Box 16443
  Charlotte, NC 28297
  Phone: 707-875-6521

- Raptor Rehabilitation and Propagation Project,
  Inc.
  Tyson Research Center
  Box 193
  Eureka, MS 63025

- Raptor Research and Rehabilitation Program
  College of Veterinary Medicine
  1988 Fitch Drive
  St. Paul, MN 55108

- Vermont Raptor Center
  Vermont Institute of Natural Science
  Church Hill
  Woodstock, VT 05091

Jobs for Writers
Writer's Digest Books
9933 Alliance Road
Cincinnati, OH 45242

Index

INDEX

. . .

·
2 8 7